Straight Talk for Principals

Raymond E. Lemley

A ScarecrowEducation Book

The Scarecrow Press, Inc.

Lanham, Maryland, and Oxford

2003

A SCARECROWEDUCATION BOOK

Published in the United States of America
by Scarecrow Press, Inc.
A Member of the Rowman & Littlefield Publishing Group
4720 Boston Way, Lanham, Maryland 20706
www.scarecroweducation.com

PO Box 317
Oxford
OX2 9RU, UK

British Library Cataloguing in Publication Information Available

Library of Congress Cataloging-in-Publication Data

Lemley, Raymond E., 1937–
  Straight talk for principals / Raymond E. Lemley.
    p. cm.
"A ScarecrowEducation book." Includes bibliographical references.
  ISBN 0-8108-4615-2 (pbk. : alk. paper)
  1. School principals. 2. School management and organization. 3. Leadership
  I. Title.
LB2831.9 .L46 2003
371.2'012—dc21   2002013194

♾ ™ The paper used in this publication meets the minimum requirements
of American National Standard for Information Sciences—Permanence of
Paper for Printed Library Materials, ANSI/NISO Z39.48-1992.
Manufactured in the United States of America.

Contents

Acknowledgments

I think ideas that find a way into writing come from many, many sources. The ideas and the words used to express them come from experiences, separate and gathered together. I realize as I reflect upon a career as a principal and educator that several people have provided an impetus to explore my thoughts and feelings about the principalship. During that time, I had the wonderful fortune to hang around with exceptional people who have influenced my thinking.

First, I want to thank Mary Lee Howe, my incredible wife and partner, who over time has guided me to a more provocative view of education. I also want to thank her for giving me such loving support and such thoughtful and valuable counsel.

John McGavack has been a friend and a mentor during most of my years as an educator. I met him in 1968 at Wilbur Cross High School in New Haven, Connecticut. He took a chance in 1972 when he hired me as the principal of Daniel Hand High School in Madison, Connecticut. I may have taken a risk accepting the job, but his was the bigger risk. Working for him paid me incredible benefits. John was the leader we all need to work for. He supported his principals and valued them for what they achieved in their schools.

The faculty and friends at Daniel Hand High School nurtured me to become an effective principal and mentor. The teachers and the students shaped my thinking about what makes a good school. So many of them remain friends today.

My colleagues at the Connecticut Association of Secondary Schools defined early on the meaning of collegiality and support so needed by any principal. David Larson, who has moved along to other responsibilities, has been an especially good friend.

Scott Thompson, the former executive director of the National Association of Secondary School Principals, gave me an opportunity to learn about how principals should be trained and about how they should be selected. He hired me to join with those developing the best assessment process ever used in education.

As the editor of the NASSP *Bulletin*, Tom Koerner demonstrated kindness and certainty in communicating. Years ago he gave me a book that redirected my point of view and set me off on a newly defined and exciting course of inquiry and thinking about leadership and about the tasks facing a principal.

My friend Noel Clark and the men and women from the former Ontario Public School Teachers Federation demonstrated incredible collegiality, showing me the way principals and teachers work for common purposes in meeting students' needs.

Julian Shaddix, the former executive director at the Texas Association of Secondary School Principals, and a member of the board of directors at the Texas Principals Leadership Initiative, provided me an introduction to many good friends at the Texas Regional Service Centers. These colleagues helped get TPLI off the ground. Julian was for me a great model of an ethical leader.

Over the past thirty years, I have had conversations with hundreds of principals and assistant principals across the country. All those words, those exchanges of ideas, helped me put this book together. So many schools in so many places benefit from the leadership of the principals who shared themselves and their words with me. I thank them. I surely hope others thank them as well.

Ray Lemley
Marco Island, FL
August, 2002

Introduction

Of all the jobs in education that I have ever held, none was more challenging and enriching or as much fun as being a school principal. I learned so much on the job. I progressed from arch amateur to a somewhat accomplished practitioner with the help of lots of fine educators and wonderful colleagues. In that incremental march toward growth, I gathered from my professional experiences some thoughts and beliefs that I was itching to set down on paper.

My reflections found voice in this book because my tenure as a principal produced a series of very strong recollections on the wonder of education. I kept discovering new twists in the paths that some eager and motivated people shared with me. Thus, this book is as much about a particular journey as it is a simple how-to book. I wrote this book because I believe that the principalship is the most vital job in education. I believe that the position is filled with good, dedicated, and talented men and women who get little acknowledgment for what they do. Principals today keep on keeping on and doing the job because for them being a principal fulfills a calling and honors a vocation that is of itself the most worthwhile task a professional can perform.

When I decided to write this book and bumped against the issues of writer's block and producing coherent simple sentences, I was motivated by thinking I had something to say. I guess that motivation struck me a few years ago when I started noting interesting themes, issues, and topics principals needed to think about. I never had any desire to craft a methods text; lots of valued colleagues have already done that and have done it quite well.

I suspect that my ambition was to express myself about some of the things that had gripped me over my forty-year tenure as an educator. Having been a high school teacher, a college English instructor, a curriculum specialist, a high school principal, a professor in an educational administration program, and an executive for two educational associations, I honestly thought I had something to say. As my thoughts took form, I realized that I had a very specific audience in mind. I was writing my list of observations and the notes that went with it for my principal colleagues.

My ego is not so large that I have any illusions about this book. It is not nor will it ever be any great shakes as a professional publication when I compare and contrast it with some other great books (see the bibliography). It may be too subjective, too personal. I am bold enough to think that it is a book about leadership. It's a field guide to being a leader in a school. If this book addresses leadership, it's because I am addressing ground level concerns that are part of being a principal. Principals are my subject and my audience.

So the content of this book is what it is because I needed to get my views set out before my peers as a way of telling them I care about what they do. I want to make a plea on behalf of principals, assistant principals, and those who aspire to the job of school leader. The plea is that we all do the job as well as we can, that we dedicate our efforts to the well-being and the welfare of the teachers and students who look to us to lead them carefully and lovingly. It is a plea to thwart the efforts of anyone whose agenda is to dismantle public education in favor of some untested fad. It is a plea that all school leaders join forces to sustain and maintain the free, open, public education that was established for the common good.

1

Engage Passionately with All That You Do

Passion is enthusiasm tinged with boundless energy and commitment. There is probably little that takes the place of a passionate commitment to the things we choose to do. You always know when you are in the presence of a leader driven by a passion for what he or she does. You just cannot ignore the feelings of a person who has passion. Think for a moment about a mentor, about that person who captured your heart with expressions of dedication to the task. It may be difficult to list the behaviors and the feelings possessed by a passionate leader. But you certainly know those feelings and that you are affected by those feelings. Passion is noted in its results.

So how does one act passionately? What might be the hallmarks of passionate leadership? I am going to make a stab at a few things one might consider in thinking about passion for the principal's job. I need to give more than a slight nod to Tom Peters and his pals who have put together some really good books that today seem forgotten. So here goes. A leader brings passion to the job by doing some of the following:

- Being enthusiastically possessed by the assignment. I am not talking about being a workaholic. I am talking about loving what you do and having very few bad days.
- Having a sense of joy about life and life's tasks.

- Demonstrating an active and heartfelt concern for the staff. That means staying close to them while they do what they do. If you are passionate about your school, then you will stay really close to what your school does; your school teaches students.
- Refusing to see problems as "their problems." That means accepting ownership for all that happens in the building.
- Carrying on a love affair with the students. Now that's an interesting premise. But how does one bring anything less than passion to a regard for the students? I do not get any of that indifference thing. It's hard sometimes to like what some of the kids do, but you can always find something in a kid to love. And that's what passion for students is all about.
- Getting really close to the community. I am talking about welcoming the moms and the dads openly into your world as a principal. I am asking my principal colleagues to troll for clients, to get out there and convince the moms and the dads that you and your staff are dedicated only to what is good for them and for their children.
- Anticipating the next worst thing and preventing it. That takes foresight, wisdom, and stamina. But it sure is a display of passionate regard. A sense of anticipation really means reading the signals, knowing what the threats and the dangers might be, and acting to keep all the bad stuff at bay. Why? Because you so love your school and the people there, it is unacceptable to let anything bad happen.
- Paying attention to the small issues in your school and staying with the resolution of small issues until they are truly resolved. Acting fanatically about the small issues is a very proactive form of quality control. Quality control is what distinguishes the pretty good product from the smashingly successful and fantastic product.
- Never downplaying some issue facing a teacher or a student. You are the supporter. You will provide the direction and the right way to get it all done. The passionate leader is the champion of those in the organization who may be having a bad day.
- Speaking truth and talking straight. No lies. No compromising statements. No sexist and racist comments. Just the best words possible out of your mouth. Passion never allows things to get tainted by the negative.

- Being dedicated to making your building look good, feel good, and be good. Everything in your building has the smell of success simply because your passion for the job allows nothing else through the door.
- Urging everyone with whom you interact to get up to speed and to perform his or her best. A passionate leader keeps everyone "up" for the tasks to be done. The passionate school leader has a sense of performance art, a sense that everything that gets done in the building is touched by creativity and by artistry.
- Keeping anything that fails to meet the standard of excellence away from the school. If any of what hovers about the school is pointless, mean spirited, or dangerous, then it stays outside; it never comes into the building. The passionate leader practices passionate regard for the protection and the well-being of all touched by the school.

Passionate leaders have little tolerance for the average. The passionate leader looks for the margin of excellence in all that he or she does and in all that the teachers and the students do. I suspect that somehow passion gets close to idealism and idealism is what we need to sustain. Teaching and learning are the most ideal goals one can set. Teaching and learning define progress and advancement for our students and for public schools. Hard-driving passion will help us sustain our vision for a situation that is dramatically better than what we have right now.

2

Bring Your Best to the Job

Do you remember all the interesting things that you shared with the committee or with the individuals who interviewed you for your job when you were hired? Think for a moment. Of course, I hope they asked you insightful and probing questions, forcing you to think about all the reasons they should give you the job as principal. I ask you about your recollections of the interview to remind you about all the wonderful things you might have shared with the interviewers.

They asked you questions like "Why should we offer you the job?" This may not be exact, but for our purposes here the wording is close enough. The interviewers were trying to get at your best. They wanted to know what set you apart from all the others—at least I hope there were others—with whom you were competing. They simply wanted you to define for them what it was that made you the great one who would lead the school from where it was to where it needed to be. They wanted to know about the knowledge, the skills, and the abilities that set you apart and that made you the person of the hour. So, what were those things? What answers did you provide that describe your best?

Take a moment and think very hard about what you consider represents your best. I want you to focus on skills. I do not want you to mouth clichés like "I am a good people person." What the heck is that anyway? Nor do I need you to say, "I am a good detail man (or woman)." There are several interesting skills that make up "detail person." An outstanding baseball player does not make the team because he is a team player. He makes the team because he can consistently hit a hanging curve ball out of the park. He is on the team because he reads a pitcher's moves and knows when he can take a gigantic lead off first base. One's best is defined by possession of specific skills and behaviors that make up "seeing the big picture." Write down some specific skills, attributes, or behaviors that say to the entire world, "These are the best things I bring every day to the job."

So we need to go beyond the recollections you have and fill in the answers a bit. We need to create a list of those things constituting the best that a principal can bring to the job. You might want to pick up a pencil and make a check mark next to the items in this list that strike a chord for you. You may well recognize several items here that will get you to say, "I do that." There may be something on this list that piques your insights and suggests to you that, "Yes, that particular action does represent my best."

Take a look at the following list and see what you think. I am endeavoring to provide some benchmarks against which you can assess and evaluate your skills, attributes, and behaviors. Among a whole range of gifts, an effective principal brings to his or her job:

- The desire to perform in the best way possible
- A healthy awareness of strengths and weaknesses
- The clearest and most specific speech possible
- Absolutely gracious behavior toward everyone
- Respect for those served by the school
- A deep regard for the expert abilities of staff members
- The ability to assist those who can be mentored; the skill of getting rid of those who resist growth
- Tolerance of ambiguity
- Sensitivity to all regardless of the situation
- Refusal to be mean spirited and angry even when provoked

- Problem analysis and judgment skills that detect difficulties and keep one from making things more complex than they are
- The ability to solve a problem
- Refusal to look for the quick fix
- The desire for the best from those with whom one works
- A commitment to keeping current with trends in teaching and learning
- The ability to write well
- Boundless enthusiasm
- A broad range of interests

3

Build the School's Vision

Leaders define the vision for the group or the organization. Defining the vision is straightforward and direct. Among all the leader's tasks, one of the truly significant is to define and establish the vision. The effective leader needs to provide direction. Defining and setting direction for the organization establishes the leader's role and determines what he or she is and does. Essentially, nothing takes precedence over vision definition and vision achievement.

All the nonsense about grassroots vision building and vision maintaining is just so much talk, so much noise that passes for purposeful activity. The leader has to assume the responsibility for defining the vision, particularly as the vision–defining and vision-building process takes form and direction. The principal certainly might seek assistance and support from a committee in building the vision of the organization. There's nothing wrong with that as long as the leader recognizes the inherent challenges and potential difficulties in working with a committee to build a vision. Committees just have a hard time getting terribly focused on more abstract tasks like building a vision. Because committees struggle with consensus, they often have difficulty coping with such an abstract assignment. They want to get the task done. Vision building presents problems early in the defining stages. In the early stages the leader may have two problems: getting his or her head around the vision tasks and moving a committee in the necessary direction to get the task completed. It's not impossible; it's just very difficult. In the early stages, maybe vision defining and vision building are not a committee's functions.

The well-intentioned discussion about the organization suggests that everyone in the organization shares a responsibility for helping to define the organization's purpose or mission. Groups have long demonstrated their fatigue with staying the course simply because staying the course is hard, very hard work; they become distracted and disillusioned with vision building and vision maintenance. Most groups and committees seek the quick fix. Building and sustaining the vision are both difficult tasks and too often all the distractions just make the process nearly impossible for committees. Only a strong and effective leader assisted by the dedicated members of the organization can stay the path and sustain the vision. That is what a good and a determined administrator (read principal) will do.

So here are some things for the principal to keep in mind:

- Get a clear picture of a future condition toward which you and, of course, the organization will strive.
- Define the specific behaviors that will move your group or organization toward achieving whatever is defined and described by a striking and engaging picture.
- Once you have talked about the picture of the future condition toward which everyone needs to work, assist the members of the organization to understand what actions they need to take to move the organization. Progress toward vision attainment is defined by specific actions.
- Provide lots of opportunity to talk about where the school, the staff, the students—all of them—are going. Give everyone a clear goal about the direction the organization must take and then engage everyone in discussion about what will happen. Let everyone talk and talk and talk some more.
- Keep everyone focused upon what is achievable. Pie-in-the-sky outcomes are very nice, very idealistic. However, you must have a vision marked by results you can reach. You need to guard against frustration caused by trying for the unachievable.

- Perform some perception checks along the way. Look around. Ask questions. Get the feel for how your school is responding and behaving. Perception checks may well be answers to the following simple questions:
  - "How are we doing?"
  - "How are we feeling?"
  - "Is all this worth doing?"
  - "Do our actions and our deeds make the organization better?"
  - "Are what we do, and what we say we will do, aligned?"

These questions provide some simple checks as you move along the path toward vision attainment. Neither focus nor attention is difficult when the attraction is some meaningful quest or dream. It just takes some sustained and nondistracted effort.

4

Focus on the School's Vision

Once you establish and define a vision, you need to be relentless in your focus. Nothing else should get in the way of your progress toward the vision driving your school. Granted, a lot of distractions exist. However, the focused administrator and educator must stay the course, must keep with the program. Focus requires attention, but attention is so difficult to maintain in the presence of numerous distractions from all the things that need doing. In fact, most of what the policy wonks tell us to do might be better left undone. We need to dig in, get really stubborn, and keep saying this: "I have a vision of what the school must be; and knowing what the school must be, I need to maintain control of the educational vision of the school."

Warren Bennis asserts that attention through vision is one of the significant attributes of leadership. When the vision is clear and the goals are specific, one can be polite in responding to any silliness that distracts from vision attainment. Here's how it works: "I'm sorry, but that issue (name one) is not right now part of our vision. Here's a copy of what we are presently focused on. Maybe when we have refined this vision and achieved some of our goals, we can give you some time. But right now our vision is all that matters."

Let us disengage from so much of the nonsense about the school's noninstructional and noneducational responsibilities. Take all the distractions somewhere else and reach for some of the higher ground. All the glib talk about "zero tolerance" sounds like someone just discovered something new and exciting. Anyone who has observed a reasonably effective school with a reasonably effective program knows that those who are truly in charge, the teachers and principals, have always had zero tolerance for stupid and antisocial behavior. So much of the current buzz in education distracts the focused and committed educators from the real tasks associated with focusing on the vision. Of course, a major part of any school's ethos is reflected in having a safe school. Absolutely, let's have high-achieving test takers. Of course we need strong attendance and behavior policies; absolutely right. We do want to reach out to students and encourage students to respect each other and respect their teachers and their administrators. We definitely require dedicated and involved parents.

However, all these "things" are preexisting conditions in an environment where a vision might thrive. What we need is less distraction created by political agendas that get adults elected to boards. The policy and legislative people have little sense of what the school's vision might be. Actually, they often have little regard for the school's vision. The principal is the keeper of the flame. Everyone and everything that keeps us away from vision achievement may play the role of educational window dressing.

Let's remove the distractions. Then the policy makers, the superintendents, can hold the principals directly accountable for vision attainment. No vision attainment, no ongoing contract. Yes, it certainly sounds much easier than it really is. However, I and others may well have the sense that expending excessive energy upon the vision and all that surrounds the established vision may put the important school business on track. Boundless effort put toward vision attainment may raise the test scores, may keep the school safer, and may keep our students in their classrooms.

We need to become less tolerant of anything that gets in the way of achieving the school's vision. Part of that vision relates to the need to provide a safe, sane, and literate environment. This is not day camp; it is school. Right on! We need not waste time with instructional programs relating to safe use of weapons—now there's an oxymoron. We do not need shooting courses. We need courses that make our young people intellectual straight shooters.

So we need to:

- Discover a vision that is a picture of something down the road that is significantly better than whatever we have right now. Although schools are much better than the harsh educational critics would have us all believe, the conditions are still not as good as they need to be. And it is not because of a lack of trying. Rather, it is because of a lack of focus. It is also the result of all the bleating from those who would destroy and dismantle free public education. I have yet to meet an other-directed, altruistic home schooler. All the alternative school missionaries are trying to run their egos over the public schools. Here's the word: Public schools with great and solid visions, with excellent principals and teachers, with a supportive community, are unbeatable. End of argument.

- Put all our efforts and all our resources toward the achievement and development of that splendid picture of the future condition. This is where reality will get tested. Let's stop wasting our time with the misguided experiments. We are up to the oarlocks in poor results. We definitely know what works when it comes to running schools. However, most of those who lead need to do it better, do it with more passion, and do it with the support of the community.

- Recognize that those who say they support schools really need to pass the support test. Support comes all the time, not just at election time, and support requires more than lip service. We need to make all the faculty teachers of the year. Is that too difficult? I think not. We already have principals working hard to support what happens in their schools. We need the parents and the community to support education.

Free public education is a supportable bargain. Forget the home schooling fringe. Yes, there have been some successes. Big deal! Public schools have an incredible record of success down through the years. There is nothing remarkable about educating kids at home. In fact, there is a rather long and interesting history of schooling on a small and personal basis. So what? If the truth were told, the home school stuff is a gigantic slap in the face of free, open, and democratic public education. It certainly is no affirmation of anything that lots of people work so hard to put forward. Let us not allow home schoolers to eat up tax support for public education. If you want vouchers and home schooling, then write a check and get your hands out of the taxpayers' pockets.

One other thing: Let the leaders of public education stop saying nice things about vouchers, home schooling, and all the other inane experiments that diffuse our vision of free, public, tax-supported education. The talk about home schools, vouchers, choice, and other experiments is interesting, but it rubs against the grain of a very sound democratic principle relating to the inscription on the Statue of Liberty. You see, the tired and the poor have always been welcomed in public schools. The public school program is driven by commonweal concepts thought beautiful and productive by our founding fathers and mothers. Anyone who supports programs other than free, public, open education should not be on the board or speak for those who honor what the schools achieve.

- Drive away any and all who fail to discern the value of the school's established vision. By the way, let us not forget that most educators desire only the good for kids in schools. We must rid the system of those who do not adhere to that truth. Forget about tenure! You fail to follow the vision, you fail to support kids and fail to treat them well, then you fail and you're gone! Now there's a "zero tolerance" policy that may have an impact.

Here's the rule: Love what you do! Teach as though your very existence depended upon your stellar performance. Unless you are capable of superb performance, we will see you in another occupation. If the university preparation programs cannot do a better job of getting young men and women ready for the professionalism of teaching, let's drag some of the professors out of their comfortable jobs and fire them. Let's get to the source of the difficulties. Maybe those who prepare our teachers are failing miserably to work to standards and to a vision of what education in the public schools needs to be.

Once we have the vision up there in lights and once we have set the course, then we need to reward all those who are part of reaching that vision. Also we need to expunge those who are distracted and in the way of vision achievement. Get real! Get hard about what we want and need to do. No alternatives to success. Success surrounds the attainment of the vision. And let's reaffirm that all kids can achieve success if we push and prod with love and devotion for them and for the vision.

5

Live the School's Vision

What is that picture of the future condition that drives your school? What are the things that your school stands for? What activities in your school make it dramatically different from all other schools? How do all the people who come into your school realize and sustain the agenda that all must support? Simply put, what makes your school a great place? A place of learning and of joy? Right now, take out a piece of paper and write down all the things that make your school great. Anyone who writes that we have a great discipline code or a fine attendance policy needs to be admonished for being stuck dead center in an incorrect priority.

Everyone on your staff must be able to answer these questions:
- What makes this school great?
- Why do the teachers show up every day?
- What do we do that makes the children show up every day?
- What behaviors and acts define our splendor?
- What are the things we value?
- Do we teach what we value?
- Do we value what we teach?
- Do we take care of all of our children equally well?
- Do we know what the acceptable behaviors look like?

- Do we know what the unacceptable behaviors look like?
- Do we love all and serve all?

If that motto works for the Hard Rock Café, it certainly can work for a place where smart people gather together to make a school. Maybe we need to ask each teaching candidate to draw a picture of instructional success. Let's make that part of the interviewing process. Maybe each principal needs to incorporate some form of the questions above into an interview for new teachers.

Hard questions, I guess. But here's a fact: Organizations that live by what they believe do the job that needs doing. Schools that stay true to the future condition that is significantly better than what you have and where you are right now consistently serve the needs of students, of parents, of faculty, of the community. How can it be any other way? If everyone lives the vision, then we are moving, and we are not wasting our time embroiled in useless and pointless arguments, in distracting arguments over whether we use phonics or whole language, whether we allow students to say prayers or not, whether we have block schedules or some other form of scheduling.

Vision- and value-driven teaching and learning are politically neither "right" nor "left." Vision- and value-driven organizations are inclined to do the best that can be done for young learners and for the communities from which learners come and to which they will return. We need little data to prove that vision-driven schools are happy and effective schools. All the bean counters in the world, all the data collectors whom you could gather up, if in fact you could gather those squirrels up, could never attain the dream imbedded in a vision. All they can do is repeat the kinds of things that continue to get schools in trouble. The nonvisionary travels in a narrow orbit, as Warren Bennis points out. Most of those who tear down public schools and demean the work of public school teachers possess small minds serving small purposes and narrow agendas. Generally we know what the public school critics are against; but what are they for? The conservative outcry over testing on either the state or national level creates a purposeless agenda that will serve only short-term gains.

Here's how you live the school's vision:

- Act in ways that promote what you say you will promote. If you say you will do a thing, then do that thing. Never leave your people scratching their heads wondering what you will do next. You see, vision and living that vision promote truth in action, word, and deed.
- Lead by example. First, you promote and support the vision. Then you set out some reasonable expectations that encourage the pleasant, honest, trusting staff members. Talk straight and be honest. Say those things simply and directly. No edubabble! Compromise no one and nothing. Avoid demeaning talk.
- Be a pillar. Be the rock, the solid foundation upon which the school needs to build an exciting vision. One never needs to pursue some neo-Christian argument to perform great deeds, to act in exemplary ways. One simply needs a value system that builds upon playing fair, being nice, and doing no harm.
- Require all those within the organization to know the vision. Give them a quiz every now and then.
- Talk about the vision. Act out the vision. Paper the walls with the vision. Announce it daily. Stay focused on it. Remember what you know about the efficacy of repetition. You cannot simply state what you feel and then move on. You need to set out the vision and repeat its exemplars as often as you can. Talk about what the staff has done to move the school along to greatness. Accept no excuses. Move on.
- Put the solid vision descriptors in the faculty handbooks in place of all the trivial regulations and codes. The shakers and the movers have achieved their dreams and have lived the visions by constant repetitions and by holding the followers accountable. That's the ticket.
- Expect the best from the staff as they work to embody and to live the vision. Expectations raise levels of achievement. One needs no hard data to prove that point. When we ask folks to do their best and give them the resources and the support to do their best, they perform at the highest levels. Most of those who work in schools have more degrees than a thermometer.

- Give the staff blatant and overt love and encouragement in their support of the vision. They need role modeling and mentoring. They need someone who can define exacting measures of performance. The teachers need a champion. When was the last time you as the principal functioned as the champion and the cheerleader for the teachers?

- Focus on quality teaching. Maybe we need to get focused upon the art of it all. Levels of mastery define best practice, and we need to push for that. We need to be assertive—not aggressive— about mastery. We need to create vivid pictures of mastery. The effective principal needs to develop a real intolerance of "average." We will have no average teachers here. We want the superstars! That's what the vision requires. We want the absolutely high performers! And as principals we will do whatever we need to do to attract and support the high fliers, the top performers. No one here simply squeaks by.

- Reward vision-enhancing behaviors. Stop wasting time with those who fail to live up to expectations. Never mind spending anything on those who fail to see clearly what they need to do. We have wasted too much time and too much effort on the "artificials," those who seem forced into the behaviors that constitute good teaching and good organizational behavior. Quit protecting the vision busters and the kid haters. Stay focused on the vision attainers, the dream catchers, and those who do exactly what they are paid to do—teach in a positive, loving, and compassionate way. Spend lots of time talking about what constitutes effective teaching. Paint pictures of effectiveness. Reward it.

    Stop worrying about comments that suggest you favor the high performers. What a bunch of nonsense. Of course you favor the high performers. Why would anyone question your spending time with the high performers and encouraging them to higher levels of performance? The low performers need to seek employment and support in other places. Actually, a vision-focused organization has little tolerance and regard for the low-performing staff members. And it was ever thus.

6

Define and Lead the Culture in Your Organization

The cultural leader defines the purpose and the vision of the school in terms of rich metaphors. Certainly those rich metaphors describe and delineate a culture. When schools are forced to struggle to maintain success, they lose the edge presented and defined by rich metaphor. Rich metaphors are what we talk about and how we talk about the incredible things that happen in our organization. The language builds upon a lexicon of attainment and success. In a rich culture, no one, particularly the leader, has any tolerance for negative language, language that demeans or lessens achievements. We talk about gains, wins, and successes. And we talk about our gains and our wins not because we have over-riding egos that flaunt what we are about. Rather we talk about our wins because our language hopefully builds striking verbal pictures that point our faculty and our students toward success and achievement. "Well, you should not get too cocky." I guess not. However, in a culturally rich school you must talk honestly about the successes you have and about the gains you make.

Thus the language of the cultural leader and the language of the organization enmeshed in a rich culture avoids some of the common linguistic references that seem to have gained popularity. In a culturally rich school, no one would ever say, "You never know what it's like unless you have been in the trenches." What kind of statement is that? Of course, the use of "trenches" forces us to visualizations like the trenches of no-man's-land during World War I. How's that for a thriving metaphor of success? Trenches bespeak destructive conflict.

No doubt, some of the naysayers and negative people do see contemporary education as fraught with peril and destructive behaviors. Better we get those commentators out of the way quickly. Those who talk about the trenches in describing schools have no constructive and vital thoughts about our children and about their well-being. Those who use the metaphor of the trenches see schools as conflict-ridden places lacking purpose and vitality. Not our schools! Not under our leadership and tutelage. Another point: When anyone describes the schools in combat language, that person is setting up the listeners to understand just why he cannot do the required job. "Look, I just told you how difficult it all is. It's crazy in there." Translation: How can I possibly be successful, even if I am a babbling fool with little or no talent?

Other common misapplications of metaphoric language are terms like "the front lines," "the combat zone," "it's a daily battle," "it's a jungle in here," and other interesting metaphors that address perceived struggle and turmoil. Not a very pleasant cultural setting or description. Cultural leadership embodies the best and brightest view of the school and its community. Cultural richness derives from looking at leadership and its attributes in win–win metaphors. Effective cultural leadership abandons those tired clichés of leadership that have been roundly put to sleep with some of the awful displays of current leadership in places like Enron, Arthur Andersen, WorldCom, and in some of our less-than-praiseworthy forms of government small thinking. One suspects that the notion of "high stakes," as in high-stakes testing, comes from our business brethren who love those win-lose metaphors designed to strike fear into one's heart. High stakes indeed!

So here are some of the attributes of the cultural leader and of cultural leadership. Think about your own behaviors and the behaviors within your school or organization as you read on.

- The cultural leader articulates the vision and the purpose of the school. The vision and the purpose of the school need to be grasped and articulated in terms that transcend test scores and high-stakes behaviors. By the way, just what is high-stakes anything?
- The cultural leader defines the values that reflect the purpose of the school. So answer these questions:
  - Can you articulate the values that reflect the purpose of your school?
  - Is the purpose to foster great thinking?
  - Is it to bring together the best that there is from the young men and women in the schools?
  - Is it to promote greatness in thought and action from everyone? Just what is it?
  - Or is it to have a great discipline code? An enforceable dress code? To win the testing game?
  - What are the transcendent values that we strive for daily in our school?
- Those who buy into the culture of the school socialize others to the values and to the purpose of the school. You are then obligated to make certain that all the staff, all the students, and the entire community served by the school understand the purpose of the school. Get really large pieces of poster paper and write on each piece, "We are here because we . . ." Never lose the chance to tell anyone whom your school touches why your school exists. By the way, it does not exist to get kids into college. Nor does it exist to make students ready to assume a job. We need to move our students to higher aspirations than the median job market niche. All those who insist that schools exist to produce job-ready employees have totally missed the transcendent mission of our public schools. In the margin right now pencil in a couple of reasons why you think that your school exists.
- The cultural leader talks about what makes the school he or she leads unique. So you need to emphasize what defines the unique character and nature of the school. Identifying the unique things in your school may take some concentration and hard work.

Uniqueness is a stretch under the easiest of circumstances. When you attempt to set your school, your kids, your staff, and yourself apart, you must focus and work at your creative best. Bring together some of your hotshots and work on this question: What sets our school apart from all others? It needs to be something transcendent. Test scores are not transcendent. High-stakes testing never was nor will it ever be a transcendent vision.

- The cultural leader develops the reinforcing symbols for the school. Do you have a special handshake? Where is the school banner placed? Do you flaunt the school colors? Do staff members other than the coaches get shirts and sweaters that tell who or what they are? Do you teach everyone how to sing the school song? Do you even have a school song? Do you have a school motto and do you use it as often as you can? Does the day commence in some significant way? Do you sing the national anthem? Are there specific activities in your school that support ritual and symbolism of the students, of the faculty, of the community? Are new staff members inducted into the fold? Are new students welcomed in some special way? Is there something special about the class ring? About the honor society pin? About the varsity letter? About the school colors or the school mascot? Your answers determine the use and the application of reinforcing symbols.

- The effective cultural leader rewards those members of the organization who accept and reflect the values and the norms of the school. I know that we are now in a very touchy area. What is all this about rewarding acceptable norms and values? Who determines what is rewarded? Who selects the rewards? The cultural leader does that. He or she does the rewarding because he or she is open, honest, and supportive of solid cultural norms and values. If respect is a cultural value, then those who relentlessly show respect are rewarded. If collegiality is something we value, then anyone who demonstrates collegiality receives some acknowledgment for that particular behavior.

- The cultural leader encourages strong bonding among the people touched by the school. All right—"bonding" might be a bit of psychobabble, I admit. But you all know what I mean here. The culture of the organization should unite the staff, the students, and the parents in common goals and purposes. No one necessarily needs to be at odds with the school if the school's actions are driven by what is best for all those served by the school. Each day, those who come to this place should be united in what happens here. So what happens to the "minority reports"? Nothing happens simply because the minority reports, unless they are marked by dramatic and substantive divergence, are filed in favor of what's best for all those served by the organization.

- The effective cultural leader helps define the strong, worthwhile purpose of the school. Over and over the cultural leader persists with the statement of mission and purpose, almost to the point of being a broken record. If excellence is the operative descriptor, the leader talks about excellence. He or she describes it; draws vivid verbal pictures of excellence; rewards excellence every time he or she sees it. If the purpose of the school is to bind the community to outstanding performance in all things, then the cultural leader constantly fosters that goal and purpose. The issue here is one of redundancy and repetition. No more, "Well, I told them once what I expect." Not enough! Tell them and tell them and tell them again. Several reps. All the time.

- The cultural leader helps others understand the strong, worthwhile purposes of the school. Understanding is the result of cognition, and one arrives at cognition through exceptional teaching and profoundly effective instruction. That is what the effective cultural leader is all about. Leadership is manifest in understanding. Sir Ernest Shackleton, the Antarctic explorer, made his men believe that their purpose was to survive. There was no other purpose. His men had to sustain and survive so they could return home. The school leader needs to identify his or her mantra that contains without any question or reservation what the school is all about. We are about caring for each other! We are about achievement! We are about moving forward together! What? What is it we do? What is it we think? Once you get all that figured out, you beat at it until it is ingrained so deeply that nothing can ever take the place of the defined purpose.

- The cultural leader gets all those touched by the school to see that the school's purpose is bound by and bound to excellence. In a sense, being bound by and bound to excellence is a great way to foster the notion of no one being left behind. No one! Not one child. Not one staff member. And no one in the community. That's a huge order, but there may be no greater way to demonstrate what the school is all about. You must understand how you bind everyone to excellence, and you need to determine just how everyone will demonstrate his or her inclination toward excellence. Leaving no one behind is the result of much more than the mouthing of a cliché. Leaving no one behind is imbedded in the very fibers of the school's culture.

- The responsive cultural leader establishes a tradition of excellence if one does not exist. Building traditions takes time, no doubt about it. So every time the cultural leader catches someone doing something right, the leader jumps on that behavior and extols it to the heavens. He or she makes a big deal over the small gains, the attempts, and the successes. Ultimately everyone comes to believe and understand that achievement is the end point and that achievement is a reward all by itself. Rewards become part of the geography of this organization and success generates its own rewards. All this defines big, amazing outcomes.

Cultural leadership and the culture of the organization are embodied in the best attributes, actions, and conditions within the organization. If culture is expressed in the values, the dreams, the aspirations, the effectiveness of all touched by the school, then the culture must be honored and it must represent the best the school offers. Building a culture takes time. It is fostered by a commitment on everyone's part to raise the school and its purposes to higher levels of achievement and excellence. It is the culture that drives a successful school. Nothing is more effective than cultural identification and cultural commitment. Cultural excellence causes the school's participants to say with extreme pride, "This is my school. This is my place."

7

Go Find Talent

How are new teachers and new personnel selected for your school? Do they show up on day one and say, "Hi! I'm your new third grade teacher"? We certainly know that in many large school districts some wizard hiding in the greater personnel changing room makes the selections. In this day of "lean pickings" I suspect that many principals are ecstatic to get a warm body. No doubt the ranks of candidates for the teaching jobs have thinned drastically. But we still contend that only the lazy principals keep saying, "I guess we need to be happy with what we can get." Wow! Certainly not the reaction of a school leader who possesses even a marginal vision for the greatness of his or her school.

The principal must identify and hire talented candidates. The task belongs to no one else; the principal staffs his or her school. Never mind all the noise about district size and district responsibility. Look: If the man or woman who gets the candidates must mentor, assess, and evaluate the new hires, then he or she needs to be in the front of the selecting line. If the principal is required to work with the new teacher, then the principal gets to select the new teacher. How else does one build responsibility? Does all that higher-level support and mentoring activity come from the fact that this warm body just walked into your building? I am afraid not. It derives from a commitment to the one you hire. Amen to that. No doubt talent always beats a lack of talent, but the issue for so many principals rests upon the ways and the means of locating talented candidates for one's school.

Consider the following strategies and suggestions about becoming one's own "head hunter."

- Develop and nurture a network of professionals who know how to find the talented candidates. Your key resource may be the local college or university that prepares candidates. I know that under-graduate and graduate programs take an awful rap these days, but maybe all the shouting is just so much scapegoating. When all else fails, the local college or university becomes the target. Call the dean or the director of the teacher preparation program. Invite yourself to the college to talk about your needs. Develop as key associates a group of professionals who teach teachers. Tell these people about your needs. Ask the preparers to visit your school. Do whatever it takes to place your school and its professional needs front and center with the teachers of the teachers.

- Whenever you attend a meeting, talk with your colleagues about your short- and long-term staffing needs. Encourage serious discussion about prospective teachers and about teacher candidates. Don't just complain about the problem. Seek solutions to the shared scarcity. Ask your colleagues where they look and what they require in a candidate.

- Develop a cadre of "master teachers" in your building whom you groom to accept student teachers. Get together and lay out the responsibilities for the master teacher. Remind them that having the student teacher is not an occasion to spend more time in the faculty room. Develop the protocols for the master teachers and get together with them frequently to see how things are moving along with their charges.

- When you receive your student teachers, look at them as can-didates for a job in your school. When the student teachers arrive in your building, define your expectations for effective participation in your building. Function as the master teacher for the master teachers.

- When you have student teachers in your building, create situations where each one of them feels welcomed into the community of professionals. Use those events and those occasions as times to celebrate effective teaching for the benefit of student teachers and new staff.
- Protect your prospective and new talent from the negative elements in your building. Make certain that the school's staff understands the operant definition of effective, wholesome, and happy participation in teaching and learning in your building.
- Encourage any talented candidate to seek employment in your district and in your school. Work with the personnel office to develop strategies that "entice" teacher candidates to look at your district or school as a great place to work.
- Make certain that you are in charge of the selection process for teachers. Never allow anyone else to make decisions that affect your school and your community. Get all of the procedures and the protocols squared away with those who assist with the task of identifying and hiring new teachers. Make certain that the personnel staff clearly understand your staffing expectations for your school.
- Use your network of the most talented teachers in the building to help with finding and interviewing prospective talent for your faculty. Quickly forget all the nonsense about who is or is not represented on the interviewing and screening committees. What you need most are very bright and gifted staff who recognize talent when they see it. Never put the "strange ones" on the committee; they recommend people like themselves. You do not need some bozo from the central office simply because someone who loves representation thinks it's good to have a central office person on the screening committee. Keep in mind that central office (whoever that is) might just send the person with the lowest IQ just to get even with you. You need no policy about screening committees. You need individuals who are committed to the success of your school and to its vision. You need talented professionals who know talent and will serve well as mentors for the new teachers you hire.

- Probe for responses from the new talent that provide you data about how smart these new guys and gals really are. Forget the old, tired, and often stupid questions about how the interviewees might respond to a riot in the cafeteria. Who cares? By the way, if there is the possibility of such incidents, do not let the new guys know that riots are commonplace in your building. Ask these teacher candidates questions that will rattle around in their higher brain centers. Ask them questions that reveal their passions and their love and respect for children. Ask them about their ability to be collegial, supportive, and loyal. Get down to the nitty gritty of teaching and learning and how all that gets accomplished.
- Say as little as possible as you interview the new talent. Refrain from telling stories about how great things were when you started out. Mark Twain reminded us all that it is a terrible death to be talked to death. Ask your questions, define your expectations, sit back, and absorb.
- Forget all the propaganda about "twofers." These are folks who can fill two slots. And in the days of budgetary craziness, you may be encouraged to make certain that you can get a coach or a second subject from the candidate. Hire people for their primary skills. If the candidate can do something else, all the better. You are seeking ways to enhance the instructional team.
- Above all else, find candidates who are qualified to teach what needs to be taught. I know that may sound silly and patronizing, but too often principals seeking a warm body hire a person who lacks the subject matter qualifications to be in the assigned classroom. Hold out as long as you can before you make things difficult for yourself.

You need to take the time to move forward with the right people. Who are the right people? Well, sometimes it may be difficult to determine just who they are. Maybe the following questions will help you and those who help select staff.

- Does this person express his or her love for kids?
- Does the candidate express his or her desire for the job in strong and specific language?

- Does this man or woman with whom you are speaking have passion? Or are you absolutely bored to death conducting this interview?
- Is this a person who will do things right? Who will do the right thing?
- How does your potential teacher express himself or herself? What are the words he or she uses? Is the language rich and metaphoric? One of the great linguists once said that how you speak is how you are.
- Are you looking at a potential role model and mentor?
- What does the package look like? Get at that appearance issue. Is the candidate dressed professionally? Does he or she act poised, mature, and confident? Is he or she articulate? Thoughtful? We know that people act how they look, and if that sounds loaded, let someone else help find the talent.
- Do you have a team player here? Mavericks are fun, but they have an overwhelming sense that they have the true light. Maybe it's just a glimmer. Watch it! The mavericks too quickly become incredible pains in the neck.

I suspect that some schools are in such desperate shape because someone has brought in teachers who are unequal to the task or unprepared. I am unclear whether it is better to fill the vacancy with a sub until the real talent shows up or to hire some light-headed person with a detectable pulse. I go for the sub simply because the union and other organizations will circle the wagons around the dumb hire. No one seems to want to get rid of the instructionally inept. It is so much easier to decry your hiring the weak teacher.

Make strong hires your mission. Get out and find the best people. Look for energetic, bright, committed candidates who will always do their very best for the students in your school.

8

Focus on the Tasks Your Teachers Need to Perform

Teachers teach. The realization of the school's vision derives from teachers teaching. And that is the focus that effective principals need to emphatically extol and enforce. How is that done?

- Define specific instructional objectives for teachers.
- Make certain that teachers have effective instruction at the center of their behaviors.
- Support those teachers who maintain their focus upon instruction.
- Get rid of those teachers who want to do something other than teach.
- Reward achievement by teachers.
- Maintain the talk and the conversation about how important teaching and learning are. Use lots of repetition.
- Make certain that all the staff talk a lot about what they teach.
- Provide the teachers with the necessary resources to do the job.
- Get the teachers involved in staff development activities that focus upon teaching.
- Support paying teachers very good salaries.
- Stand back and watch things happen.

Welcome to the age of distraction. Enter any school today and you will encounter such a range of activities that you might begin to question the intent and the purpose of what goes on in the school. The public, for some deranged reason, has developed a set of expectations that permits, in fact encourages, distractions in school. The public expects that the schools will unquestionably take care of everything . . . *absolutely everything*. No matter how you plead with the constituencies, they may very well distract you from the essential mission that ranks at the top of the agenda—to teach kids and to do the absolute best to help kids learn. A declaration that the primary purpose of schools is to teach children is often greeted by a response that teaching is an antiquated agenda, an unhip purpose that conflicts with more sexy items like enhancing self-image, maximizing potential, transitioning to the workforce, vocationalizing, and socializing—all more engaging than plain teaching. Teaching is very difficult. Transitioning is . . . well, it is just nonsense.

All the distractions seem to be defined by a kind of eduspeak that fails to be properly translated into specific teaching and learning tasks. And we have discovered an array of camouflaged words to mask the insidious distractions that take us away from teaching. The new eduspeak talks about "enhancing," "promoting self-awareness," "sharing," "networking," "modeling," and other assorted activities. None of these notions is entirely wrongheaded. The failure lies in forgetting that teaching and learning take precedence over self-actualizing. In fact, effective teaching goes a long way toward making the learner feel successful.

We get so caught up in worrying about varieties of stylish agendas that we forget that our purpose is not just to prepare kids for the workplace (it is quite all right to do that, by the way). The essential mission of schools is to prepare a young person to live a richer, fuller, and more meaningful life. It transcends flipping McDonald's burgers and goes well beyond the most recent changes in computer applications.

It takes less skill to sit around and talk pretty talk about self-image than to grind away at the difficult concepts imbedded in a rigorous subject like math or physics or reading. The argument that students do not elect to pursue the more rigorous courses is bogus.

Increasingly, we are aware of the merit of rigor in the courses taken by young students. The adults need to give purpose to more rigor. Teachers and parents need to demand that kids do the hard stuff. Let's just quit asking teenagers how they feel about algebra; who really cares how a fifteen-year-old feels about a hard subject? Let's encourage all the teenagers to get with the program and get smart. Forget all the idle chatter about the electronic age and the beauty of the computer superhighway. Kids still need to know how to read and how to think. We must get back to teaching young people to use their minds to form concepts that will allow them to tell that much of what appears on their computer screen and on the tube may be junk.

How many times do you have to tell staff members that they need to return graded papers to the students? There is no compromise on that one. It's called "feedback." And everyone, particularly young learners, needs feedback. So when the staff member says, "I did not get the papers graded," then you say something like, "Grading papers is your job. So do it." Never mind all the baloney about how busy we all are and about the distractions in our lives. Teachers teach and a part of teaching is grading papers. Here's a policy statement from a real faculty handbook: "It is our expectation that teachers will mark homework papers appropriately and return them to the students in a timely and expeditious manner." What does that mean? You need to say, "Grade papers accurately. Return papers promptly."

Then there's the view that teachers and administrators must support a misguided social agenda that asks them to cure all the ills defined by others. Reason suggests that teachers teach, that administrators lead and provide direction, and that mothers and fathers face and reject the nonteaching and noneducational agendas being foisted upon educators. Public school teachers should not be distracted from their purposes by drivel and distraction. Nor should we be distracted from our instructional purpose by patronizing our students with demeaning subject matter that will never challenge or excite the magic of learning hard content. We can certainly have shop classes, marching bands, tap dancing, and vocational study. We can have it all in our curriculum as long as it is built upon substantial teaching and learning.

Where does it say that teachers have the responsibility to get young people ready to take on anything that is less challenging and more boring than some of the tasks they will meet in the workplace? We keep hearing the ranting and the raving from the business community that kids with diplomas lack the skills to do the things required by the workplace. Maybe if the business community got wired into the process, having a nice pool of diploma-carrying individuals with a hearty dose of general education would satisfy them. It is not our task to make anyone workforce-ready.

It is definitely our responsibility to teach the hard concepts like truth, honor, dedication, loyalty, brotherhood, and all the difficult notions that learners need to master. A small dose of *Macbeth* will take a young person a long way in his or her understanding of honor and intrigue. Working a group of high school seniors through the great gestures of Henry V will get them to know the derivation of the concept of "Band of Brothers" and the pride in a task well completed. If you want the young men and women to be challenged and feel rewarded by resolving the challenge, give them a difficult math problem and guide their young hearts and minds to a solution. Then watch the lights go on. By the way, forgo the arguments of relevancy. We have been pursuing that useless argument for too long. If relevancy were the key issue, we would have to put the brakes on lots of school functions.

9

Pay Attention to Effective Teaching

Refuse to get sidetracked by anything that fails to mark the relationship between vision attainment and effective teaching. If you want to truly live the vision, you have to demand outstanding teaching. Nothing second rate, nothing marginal. Only the best performance daily by the "instructional staff." They are called instructional staff because they teach. That's the minimal requirement. No running around solving gossipy issues, no sticking noses in places where noses are certainly not required. Teachers teach. Administrators administer. Nothing more; nothing less.

Enough with the remediation already. Stop all the on-review nonsense with the staff. Schools are for children and for their learning; they are not places for on-the-job training. Let the inept stay in college or keep on with the internships. Stop paying for awful performance. Do you ever get the feeling that there is too much remediation in staff development? Do you have the sense that all the staff developers keep hoping that teachers will do poorly so they (the staff developers) can continue to sell their snake oil? When you ask a candidate if he or she can teach, tell that person you will give him or her one semester to establish credibility. No more! No less! That's it. One semester. Those folks you are about to hire have been working for more than four or five years to get it right.

Neither they nor we can afford the luxury of more time to develop a skill they should possess. We need to give developmental time to promote mastery and to refine the art of teaching.

One other thing: If the local college or university insists upon sending you less-than-stellar candidates, make a pilgrimage to the local college and get the professors to realize that they are doing a very poor job. Accept no excuses about who is to blame. If the higher education folks hang their hats on the notion of teacher preparation, let them prepare people for success. Accept nothing less. Maybe the first few interview questions need to be addressed to the university preparation people. The first question is: Do you honestly believe that the man or woman I am about to hire is ready to assume responsibility for several dozen young minds? Give me a simple "Yes" or "No."

Perhaps the teacher you have hired from the local college or university should come with a money-back guarantee. It would work this way: I will hire this candidate. If the candidate fails to teach well within the first two months, I will return the teacher to your campus and you will make him or her ready. In the meantime, you will provide me the funds to hire someone to take the place of the inept one I just hired and for whom you provided strong recommendations. Sounds like that process might have some telling consequences. All in favor please send me an e-mail.

One last notion: What is all this about "on review"? What exactly does that mean? Why do the teacher associations and the teacher unions talk about retrofitting poor performance? Why should we subject nice students to poor teacher per-formance? Why do we allow poor teachers to waste the time of young learners as the teachers acquire skills they should have to begin with? I often think of remedial piloting. The airlines hire pilots who seem not to have it quite right. So they tell these poor pilots they can practice on planeloads of people with the hope they will achieve excellence in landing. Does that sound rather silly? Well, we do the same thing by putting inept people in the classrooms.

Here are some indicators of competence. I want you to add to this list any time you feel the urge to do that. Write in the margins your "look fors" for effective teaching.

- Teaching a lesson that has a coherent beginning, middle, and end.
- Demonstrating knowledge in the subject (mastery is even better).
- Mastering effective classroom control.
- Getting from the beginning to the end of the lesson, the unit, the term without any major mistakes.
- Engaging and involving the learners.
- Possessing a command of the spoken and written word.
- Practicing strong reinforcement skills.
- Demonstrating love of what he or she is doing.
- Correcting errors and reinforcing correct responses.
- Keeping the learners focused upon the learning.
- Possessing a commanding presence.
- Being a nice person.
- Loving the students and the subject.

Now this is really a rather simple and straightforward list of skills and abilities. It is pretty basic and essential to a minimal effort on the part of the teacher. After these skills and abilities are demonstrated and mastered, everything else is downhill. You need to observe these skills as part of your assessment of the teacher. If the teacher lacks these skills, you probably need to get rid of the teacher. Start over.

Being an instructional leader implies skills on your part. You get the title of instructional leader if you know a lot about teaching and learning. One of the most essential skills you can bring to your position as principal and instructional leader is your gift of identifying great, even good, teaching. There are so many lists of indicators of effective teaching. Some of the assessment models for examining teaching are yours for the taking. But the skill of discerning really inspired teaching is to sit in the presence of the teacher and have sort of an "attaboy" response. You know what you are watching is great because what you see has an incredible impact on you as you sit there absorbing the greatness of the instruction. It's not marginal. It's not average. It does not get a "3" on your old 5-point grid. It knocks your socks off, and you come away from the engagement with this master teacher with a sense of wonder. What you feel right then and there is what you need to feel every time you get in front of the onrushing elegance of incredible instruction. And it needs to happen every day in every classroom.

You are responsible for getting those wondrous results. That's your job. Your job should never be defined by your skills in maintaining the budget. How's this for an inscription on your headstone? Here Lies a Great Budget Builder. Boy, oh boy! That sends shivers down my spine. As you reflect upon your professional goals you probably need to write, "I must seek perfection among my faculty in instruction." Now you can get the team jacket for the Instructional Leadership Olympics. You made it.

10

Be an Instructional Leader

We have had lots of discussion over the past few years about instructional leadership and what it means to be an instructional leader. Probably the Association for Supervision and Curriculum Development has done as much as any group to move the instructional leadership agenda into the forefront. ASCD has published several good "guides" for the practitioner about what instructional leadership is and about how to do it. For the richer and fuller exploration of instructional leadership, you need to visit one of ASCD's bibliographies on this topic.

Instructional leadership is really at the core of what principals do or should do. The problem is that instructional leadership may be difficult for principals. Many principals feel a bit intimidated by curriculum issues. Many of us understand the feeling expressed in comments like, "Well, I was a middle school math teacher. What do I know about irregular verbs in Spanish?" Or, "I taught fourth grade. Talking about seventh grade social studies is really challenging." These are true expressions of concern. However, they express false misgivings about instructional leadership and become rationalizations for principals' not asserting their instructional leadership behaviors. No one needs to have mastered the fifth declension nouns in Latin to discuss what needs to happen in a foreign language class. Nor does anyone need to have written a lesson plan in Advanced Placement Physics to know what the physics class looks like as it moves along effectively.

Instructional leadership hangs upon some rather basic considerations for the principal. A principal needs to stay focused upon the teaching and learning in his or her building. Here are some tips that may represent basic behaviors for the instructional leader. The principal needs to do particular sets of things and needs to stay focused upon those behaviors to display the skills of an instructional leader. Here's what an instructional leader does:

- Spends time talking about teaching and learning in the school. Interactions with teachers are marked by talk about teaching and about what makes for good and effective instruction. At the very least, every principal should ask several teachers each day, "How did the class go?"
- Expresses enthusiasm for the instruction that takes place in the classrooms. The instructional leader is the passionate spokesperson for the best instruction possible.
- Knows how to talk about teaching and learning. Think about this one for a minute: What are the words that signal your interest in teaching and learning in the classroom? Develop a list of key words and phrases and use the words from that list a lot.
- Knows the look of effective instruction. Can you tell good teaching from bad teaching? There is a difference, and instructional leaders know the difference. The instructional leader has in his or her head and heart a set of teaching skills (no matter how small) that facilitate good teaching. In the margin right now note three or four skills that create the picture of good teaching. "Maintains good discipline" may not be a good start for the instructional behaviors.
- Demonstrates his or her ability to teach well. Wow! You mean to say that an instructional leader needs to teach well? Yes, I do mean that. The instructional leader has to be a master teacher. So if you are shaky in this area, get some coaching and rebuild your instructional mastery.

- Gives clear feedback after a classroom visit. What does it mean to say, "You do not hold your students to standards." Can you translate that into specific language? If a teacher is to grow, that teacher needs your feedback expressed in very specific language.
- Makes certain that every meeting agenda contains items devoted to teaching and to learning. This is very important. Here's something we know for certain: A person talks about those things that are important to him or her. Right? So if you never talk about teaching and learning at a faculty meeting, what conclusions do I as a teacher draw from the fact that instruction never finds a way onto your agendas? Is it not as important as bus schedules? Principals often talk a lot about bus schedules and other such issues. If the core issues are instructional, then talk instruction. Talk learning. Let the noninstructional leaders manage the other issues.
- Can translate the generic term "accountability" into specific behavior. Now this is interesting. The policy wonks have not a clue about what accountability means. And yes, I am picking on them. But as an instructional leader, you need to know what accountability in the school looks like. Here are some accountability behaviors:
  ○ Provides students with specific feedback
  ○ Returns papers quickly
  ○ Is always prepared
  ○ Teaches every minute of the instructional period
  ○ Has well-prepared lessons
  ○ Teaches every student
  ○ Describes mastery levels to his or her students
  ○ Reinforces good learning behaviors
  ○ Serves as a cooperative member of an instructional team
- Understands the difference between management tasks and instructional tasks. This is an important distinction. Maybe the guiding principle here is, "The principal takes care of the instructional tasks; someone else does the management tasks." Now that might not be too easy. But I do not think it is too difficult. Also this might be a good time for an interesting

"paradigm shift" from the principal as manager to the principal as instructional leader.

- Ensures that the bulk of in-service activity is given to improving instruction. Not too difficult to understand. The instructional leader brings resource people into the building to talk about learning, about teaching. He or she leaves all the other fashionable topics to the district-level in-service.

- Makes certain that all staff do not waste assigned instructional time. What we do here in this building is teach. We waste little time with noninstructional activities.

- Knows how to secure central office support for instructional tasks. There really needs to be a clear understanding between the site and the central office that defines what everyone in the school does. The adults in my building teach. Central office never interferes with that. Central office exists to serve the school. It is not the other way around.

- Assigns the strongest teachers to the learners with the most problems. The reward for being the best teacher is to work with the most challenging students. That's it. The effective instructional leader never gives the weak teachers the difficult kids. When the weakest teachers work with the difficult students, the students only get worse, never better. By the way, the weak teachers teaching the most challenged students get worse also. The challenge of working with difficult students does not make the weak strong, it makes them crazy.

- Spends significant amounts of time observing in the classrooms. Is this hard to understand? Look at your schedule. If at least 50 percent of the time is not allocated to being in the classrooms, you are paying attention to the wrong things. Nothing, absolutely nothing, takes precedence over time in the classrooms. If you want achievement in your school, go where the action is. Whoops! This may be another paradigm shift.

Instructional leadership is nothing mystical. It's the most grassroots, basic, ground level, and fundamental notion in schools. It seems hard and it may even be hard. It certainly is intimidating. As the principal, you have to engage in instructional leadership by meeting the teachers and the students where they live. It's their turf, and it must become yours as well. If you do not get the message about the significance of your role as instructional leader, then you will never talk the talk. You will be working the edges of the organization. The heart and the soul of the school are instruction. And instruction and all that goes with it need you as the leader.

11

Define Expectations for Everyone in the Organization

Have you ever asked this question in the face of ambiguous directions: "What do they expect?" or "What does everyone want from me?" Both of these questions are born of a frustration that all of us share with the vague, the unclear, and the imprecise, particularly in situations where a little guidance and direction might get us out of the blocks. What is even worse is when one fails to define expectations and then holds everyone hostage because that failure has created real ambiguity and confusion in the organization.

Simply defined, expectation is never to be confused with the demand that we all live and work to the rhythm of nonresponsive rules and policies. Nor is expectation defined and set by unwavering policies designed to undermine our autonomy and our ability to use creativity and common sense. The regulatory provisions of testing programs will never do anything to improve the quality of teaching. Actually, all those regulations that seem so very specific have done little to make the instructional lives of teachers and the administrative lives of principals any more effective. Nor have the regulations provided creative and energetic classrooms for young learners.

Probably one can define expectations with a rather specific and straightforward list of actions, activities, and behaviors that work for the school. Let us try this list as an example of how one defines simply and clearly the school's expectations. Now think for a minute that what follow are not rules, regulations, or policies. This is a list of what one does when one takes on the job of "teacher" in this school.

- Teach as though your very life depended upon your success.
- As the song says, "Be true to your school."
- Treat colleagues professionally. Unfair criticism—Out. Bad-mouthing—Out. Maximum cooperation—In.
- Refrain from mean-spirited conversations—about anyone and anything.
- When you need to voice a concern or a complaint, voice it to someone who can do something to fix it, to make something better.
- Return phone calls from parents quickly. No excuses.
- Don't whine about things that do not work. Work to make things better.
- Return papers to students quickly.
- Assign only what you will grade; grade what you assign.
- Always be clear in your explanations.
- Provide rich, abundant, and specific feedback.
- Be punctual for everything.
- Do not make people wait for you.
- Be nice.
- Play fair.
- Hurt no one.
- Love your students—all of them.

One need not have several advanced degrees to follow that list. Think what your school might be if everyone lived up to the expectations set out in that simple list. Actually, that list might provide the form and structure for a pretty good faculty handbook. The list might also serve as a set of benchmarks for teachers to use in evaluating their performance day to day. Not too bad. Try it. See what might happen. The potential to make things better is rather awesome.

Part of what has generated all the silly rules, policies, directives, manuals, and more regulations than you might read in several sittings is a distrust of the general definition of expectations. Expectations are formed out of the generalizations similar to those our mothers gave us when they said rather sternly, "Behave!" No need to get into the array of specific admonitions and directions. No rules and no policies needed here. We all knew what was required in meeting the expectations laid out by Mom when she cast that look and said, "Behave." No need for lots of filling in the blanks. When she said, "Behave," we knew the behaviors imbedded in that one-word directive. The expectations were clear.

Do not simply tell teachers, students, parents, and community members what you want and what you expect; draw pictures for them. Use eloquent and colorful language to paint wonderful verbal snapshots of behaviors. Help everyone on your staff to acquire and master a very specific set of expectations about what makes the organization great. You cannot simply name the expectations; you absolutely must help everyone understand what your picture of "the best" looks like. Before you knew how to do it better, you may have selected words that were not strong or concrete enough. Maybe those who heard your words failed to understand. "Well, these are professionals; they know what I am talking about." Maybe your muttering and stammering have gotten in the way of clear pictures. Listen, you are trying to get across something that is essential and vital to the effectiveness of the school. So you have to go to the big visualizers, the things that explain best. When you assert that "everyone on my staff is a professional," exactly what does that mean? What picture should teachers get in their heads about "professional"? Take a note pad and write down the specific behaviors associated with "professional." What must one do to live up to the expectations embedded in the term "professional"?

If you feel compelled to describe "professional" in a memo, then do not trust the memo unless you have spent some time working and reworking it with your best language. Fill the memo with very concrete, colorful, and exciting language. Memos are probably in the same category with junk mail. You think your memo is more special than the things that get filed in the round file? No way!

So if what you are saying is supposed to define, explain, clarify, specify, and delineate that expectation, take some time and go over it again . . . and again . . . and, yes, you got it, again.

By the way, you must believe that you do need seven to ten repetitions depending on the level of brain dysfunction of those in the audience. All of us, to some greater or lesser degree, are slightly brain dysfunctional, have a bit of ADD, or simply determine in our rather perverse way that we are not going to listen. Possibly we think we are listening and are quite distracted by all the activity that makes a school a school. After all, schools are frenetic places loaded with distractions. Maybe we decide that what the boss is saying does not apply to us. Make your point so that it applies to everyone. When all else fails, try this directive: "Go teach!"

12

Develop a Passion for Outcomes

In the effective organization led by an effective leader, outcomes are all that matter. Outcomes go way beyond the simple-minded test results. You certainly can talk about all the peripheral issues, about the latest whizbang, the newest gizmo, and the smartest widget. But outcomes are what define the worth and the value of the actions and behaviors of the organization. Outcomes are part of the dance program and the debate program for the school. Outcomes are part of the attendance record and staff tardiness records. Outcomes relate to the number of moms and dads who attend the back-to-school programs. Outcomes are far more than the results of the state testing.

One has the feeling that "outcomes" may be another way of referring to the bottom line. But it is truly more than that. The bottom line and what it suggests point to some kind of margin, some kind of profit that defines the essential nature of the work and the effort of the organization. Outcomes are all that and so much more. Outcomes have to do with the way everyone feels about what is transpiring in the organization. Outcomes have to do with the look and the feel of the organization. And outcomes are what everyone—regardless of position or function—can get relentlessly passionate over. Think about the most recent awards ceremony at your school. Visualize the face of any young woman or young man who walked across the stage in the auditorium to receive a prize for some achievement. Get a good mind's eye view of that wonderful face. Now tell us all about "outcomes."

Outcomes transcend results. Outcomes are ways of defining the transformational elements in the school. They have to do with how sparkling clean the school is, with how little vandalism exists on your campus. Outcomes are quite different from results. When you go to the doctor and get some blood work done, a couple of days later you get some results. But you do not get outcomes unless you decide to make some changes based upon the results of that series of tests. Outcomes define all the successes that the organization can experience. Outcomes are a function of vision. No cold test results ever helped redefine the vision. Test results relate to goals and objectives. Outcomes have to do with the transcendent meaning of the organization. Outcomes are why the school as an organization, as an entity, exists.

There may be nothing rational, measurable, or quantifiable about outcomes. But you sure know when you achieve outcomes. And no one will ever say, "So what?" when you announce your outcomes. Try getting the hair on the back of your neck up and itchy with this announcement: "Our reading scores have come up one stanine." Now there's a big deal. If the best we can work for is defined by stanines, then let's pack it in! Rather, we should seek to brag about how the kids read lots of books and talk literately about their reading. That's an outcome. When you sit in a history class and students talk in ways that express relationships, comparisons, contrasts, and abstract concepts, then you are talking outcomes, not test results.

So what you need to do is this:

- Set clear reference points (benchmarks) for the school's outcomes.
- Talk incessantly about what outcomes look like at your school.
- Extol outcomes that have the look and the feel of relished success.
- Encourage everyone who comes through the schoolhouse door to love solid outcomes.
- Allow no one to be cynical of wondrous outcomes.

- Get the teachers to brag about their outcomes.
- Preach and teach that outcomes are not accidents. Rather outcomes are the studied results of living the vision.

School principals have always been the champions of outcomes. None of them were suddenly awakened from sleep simply because some business guru started beating an accountability drum. One would think that effective principals and teachers never gave one thought to outcomes until "accountability" became such a huge word in the political and business world. Without any real rationale, gurus came out of the woodwork and started yapping about how education needed to become more focused upon outcomes. Where have all the experts been for the past several decades? Our schools and those who arrive daily to teach in them have never abandoned outcomes. Just a thought: Did GM's need to recall thousands of cars to fix a defect result from thinking about outcomes? Were all the experts who were shredding documents and altering financial reports thinking about accountability to their investors? Were they thinking about outcomes? Principals need not be preached to about outcomes. They need to be supported in their pursuit of wonderful outcomes.

Outcomes truly relate to vision. Remember, we called vision a picture of a future condition that looks much better than the picture we currently have in our minds. And that's what outcomes are. Outcomes need to be, must be, a picture of daily ends that make some bit of progress over the preceding day. We never stand still. We never just hold our position. As George Patton so eloquently told his officers and men, "We move forward. We never hold our ground."

Outcomes are defined by moving forward. Every principal who accepts a paycheck from the largest or smallest school district must shout about his or her expectations for exceptional outcomes. Now exceptional outcomes have little to do with some artificial benchmark that someone who has never worked with kids defines for the teachers and the principals. Exceptional outcomes derive their meaning from a constant emphasis on daily improvement. That's what principals must expect from the staff. The word needs to go out that all we expect is that every teacher in the building will do one bit better today than he or she did yesterday. It tells us that every young man or woman, every child will be one little bit better tomorrow than he or she was today.

Effective principals need to be constantly asking of their faculties, "What have you done today to make us better than we were yesterday?" That question has nothing to do with discipline and attendance codes. Often the rules and the policies create distractions that keep good educators from their commonweal purpose: to get children to be one bit better today than they were yesterday. I suspect that when we use "better" we focus upon intellectual growth first and foremost. That's the school's focus. The other forms of growth derive from intellectual growth.

Try these steps:

- Remind the faculty that they have to teach to achieve outcomes—no wasted time; no wasted efforts. Get rid of the seatwork and the homework during class time. Teach! That's how you get outcomes. Anyone here remember "time on task"?

- Stop wasting valuable time with the noninstructional nonsense! Quit the eye tests. Let the nursing staff manage and supervise that and find some way to do it so that eye exams (vision screening) stop taking away from class time. Then you will get outcomes.

- Stop and think about the daily activities. If an activity has little or nothing to do with instruction, then engage very warily. Be really jealous of time and how it is used.

- Get hard about sick time and personal days. What are personal days anyway? What's that all about? Personal days are give-ups for the board. If they do not provide decent salaries, they overwhelm the staff with give-ups. Do the students get personal days? Then why should the adults take something called personal days when the kids are there in school? Teaching is hard work, we all agree with that. Being a principal will wear you down. But if you can't do the job, go find something else to do. The only way we will get outcomes is if everyone on staff shows up to do his or her job.

13

Teach, Model, and Expect Loyalty

Loyalty these days may be running second to customer satisfaction. Maybe you wonder, as I do, what ever happened to loyalty and to satisfaction with service? Where did it go? Why is it such an old-fashioned idea? I suspect that it might be fun to hold some kind of induction ceremony for new and senior staff alike with a grand celebration of loyalty to the school. Can any of us forget the old rock and roll song, "Be True to Your School"? Now that was a poem about loyalty. But why have we lost all that? I suspect that loyalty has grown out of fashion. It is certainly unfashionable to tell anyone how much you like being part of your faculty, part of your school. When "professionals" get together, they always want to have as a part of the agenda, "Problems we are having." Let's have an agenda that talks about "Homeruns," "Smashing Successes," "Outrageous Victories." Let's have teachers write essays entitled "What I Did to Promote Loyalty in My School."

It may be that the accountability movement is built upon both real and imagined threats about what will happen to teachers and to principals if we fail to meet the accountability standards. (By the way, who is setting those standards? The instructional team in the building? The instructional leaders in the schools?) Please note that threats serve well the function of diminishing and negating loyalty.

Too many of the amateurs who populate our faculties feel they are underachieving. How can you talk about loyalty and successes when all you have been taught is to act like a whiny baby? Maybe that's what we mean when we talk about being the devil's advocate. Being an organizational baby who voices lots of wants and needs may be the fashion of the moment. How can adults operate in a world they see as needing to take care of them? How can one be loyal while griping about the lack of a phone or the lack of long distance privileges? How can one be loyal while focusing on the failure of the office staff to meet his or her needs? What happens to loyalty when complaining and moaning get in the way? It may be impossible to be loyal to an organization for which we have developed an outrageous set of expectations for our personal rather than professional care.

Loyalty has absolutely nothing to do with "playing the devil's advocate." If you want to align your dreams behind a successful organization, then you need to discover another, more friendly, deity for whom to advocate. I think that it is interesting when those with divergent reactions use that phrase about being the devil's advocate. What they are too often doing is squelching a good idea, a creative impulse, because the idea is not to their liking. It has little to do with cognitive divergence. It has a lot to do with simply refusing to get on board. Doesn't that expression get to you when all those who express uninformed and rather inane ideas tell you, "Well, I'm just playing the devil's advocate"? Let those devil's advocates get wired into the program and play the loyalty card.

Playing the devil's advocate may show that you haven't a clue about what's going on and that you are simply not bright enough to keep your silly opinions to yourself. I am not talking about the obligation to voice a perspective that says, "I think you guys are headed in absolutely the wrong direction." You see, expressions like that are loyal; cheap shots are definitely disloyal. Saints protect us from statements that begin, "I honestly want to share . . ." Some people seldom recognize honest sharing of anything, and sharing, it seems, often presents you with ideas you would never entertain to begin with. Why do some folks presume that others need to know and hear their silly opinions? Or that they need to have anything to do with sharing?

From this moment forward, we will couch and imbed our complaints, our objections, in loyalty. Here's how this all works:

- When you take on a new position as the leader of the organization, you let those with whom you will work know what loyalty means to you.

- Describe for your staff how you will employ loyalty toward your people and how you expect loyalty in return. Your first "speech" (heaven help us!) is about loyalty and why that particular virtue is important to you and to your school and to the children who attend the school.

- If you are unclear about loyalty and what it means, do not take the job. Go work as an apprentice leader and work with someone who can help define loyalty for you.

- Show everyone just how loyal you are. As the new principal (or the old one, for that matter), provide some specific and outstanding models of loyal behavior. Talk about every example of loyalty you see during your first few days at the school. Seek examples of loyalty. Describe loyal behavior for those who lack the foggiest notion of what loyalty is all about.

- Avoid bad-mouthing the board chairperson. Quit complaining about the associate superintendent. Remember Mom's advice, "If you can't say anything nice, then say nothing at all."

- When you have a problem, go to the source, to the agent provocateur, and explain what's going on with them, with him, with her that stretches and tests your loyalty.

- It is hard to sustain loyalty to dishonest participants, to disloyal individuals who want more than they are willing to give. Principals and teachers must know that they are supposed to put more into the system than they take from it. Loyal behavior looks like high performance and giving the best all the time. It means that you leave the place a lot better than it was before you arrived.

- Speak your piece honestly. No need for careless confrontation, for the "quick draw of the fast gun." However, we need to develop a leadership style that does not fear what others may say when directly confronted with the absurdity of their statements. Sorry. No more. We absolutely refuse to roll over when attacked by the less knowing, by the less informed, and by the less caring. When someone says something stupid and disloyal, avoid answers like "That might be an interesting point of view." It just may not be interesting at all, and your comment might sound condescending and patronizing. When someone says something rather stupid by way of "sharing," say nothing in response. Guess what? The uninformed quickly get the message. Many principals have had to deal with this comment: "You know, your teachers are all jerks!" Here is a fine response: "No! They are not. They are high performers who work very hard."

- Use specific, direct, and to-the-point language. Quit beating around the bush.
- Loyalty is earned, not forced by fear of reprisal. Never use recrimination to get loyalty. It will not hold.

14

Work for the Small Gains

It seems that things in schools make haste gradually. All educators know how long it takes to teach a child to read. We all know how long it takes to make a student proficient in a foreign language. So let's find some joy in the small gains. If we rejoice over the little steps our students take, they may be less reluctant to take the bigger ones. And talk about esteem!

Effective teaching and learning is often hidden in the small gains that effective teachers and principals make over time. How many of you have hired lots of new teachers? Aren't you glad when the green ones find the building the second day? Doesn't it make you smile when during the first month the new teachers stop making the silly errors on the attendance sheet? Aren't you pleased as could be when the tardy staff members finally get the word and arrive on time? All those are small gains that put smiles on the principals' faces.

Every educational policy maker has talked about the silver bullet. So many of the university folks have been arguing about the ultimate cure for the troubles and the turmoil in schools. Most of the really good solutions are discovered in the small and incremental steps, the little gains that we make by hard and relentless work. If all the great programs launched at the expense of children were so great, then why are we, after all the talk, all the research, all the defined and redefined policy, still arguing about the way to get the job done? No one really cares much about which language arts program is the best except those who write and publish textbooks on the subject. Most of the moms and the dads and the teachers care about how effectively the children learn their language arts skills. Really quite simple! Small gains move the learner toward success regardless of which program one uses.

As you think about "small gains" consider this:

- Sometimes we simply give people too much to do, too many directions at one time.
- Try this question: Do I want my people to succeed or to fail? If you want your staff to succeed, you will work for the small gain.
- Reinforcing small behaviors or small cognitive changes has ultimate payoff.
- It is much easier to reinforce and to reward that small and specific task or act.
- Most people do better when the larger tasks are broken down into the smaller tasks; they really feel more successful when they can manage the simple before they attack the more complex.

15

Make Policy Make Sense

All right, let's all go to the handbooks and the policy manuals and reread them carefully. Someone once said that we must deal with the proximate before we can effectively deal with the remote. So our policies need to handle more proximate issues. For example, an attendance policy should take care of an immediate problem: this particular student is late or absent. The attendance policy has nothing to do with his or her patterns of attendance at a job some ten years down the road, and it is delusional to think so. Get the kid to school on time tomorrow. Does the windy attendance policy do that? We need to answer some questions about close-in policy, about the policies that govern our school.

- Is this policy really necessary?
- Is the policy understandable to all people who read it?
- Does the policy resolve the problem it was designed to resolve?
- How many individuals does it take to make the policy or the procedure work?
- Can this policy be implemented and enforced by the smallest number of people?
- Does the newest person in the school understand this policy and how it works?
- How did the policy get here in the first place?

- Does this policy require a level of work that is disproportionate to the problem addressed?

Once we have asked some of these questions about the present policies, we may have an understanding of what is imposed by policy. You see, policy is supposed to make things easier, not more difficult. Policy is supposed to be an extension of a rational response to a problem. The myth of policy is that if the policy looks and sounds rational, it will make the problem go away. Doubtful assumption. Check out all the foolishness contained in attendance policies. Do any attendance policies really get the students to come to school? Maybe we should have policies that require all the teachers to be interesting and exciting. Then the kids might come to school simply because they truly like and enjoy what the teachers are doing. The kids just hate to miss the excitement. Let's have a policy that says our principals will make informed, sound decisions, and let's fire the principals who do not adhere to that policy.

We might focus on how policies are set out and never taken back. When we write a new policy, we seldom search for an old one to expunge. We add; we seldom subtract. So here's an approach and it goes like this: "I will be happy to consider a new policy that governs the way widgets are distributed to faculty; however, you must identify the policy that will be erased as the proposed one is put in place." Here's the policy on policies: "Put a new one in; take an old one out."

A rule about rules: The new one has to make something work more easily. It has to be simple and make things simple. It cannot make things more complex. One other point: The new policy must not generate paper.

Another rule about rules: The new rule has to make more sense than the old one. A corollary is that it must also be better written. And the rule should not anger people unless the rule applies to them personally.

One last comment here. (Well, you will never get one last comment in this work. There will always be something else.) When you put in a policy, it must be enforceable by anyone on the staff.

We are not going to have policies that make work only for the assistant principal. If you want kids to be on time for *your* class, let's have a policy that empowers you to make it all work. Let's have a policy that allows the newest, most inexperienced teacher to enforce the policy easily.

If you need a dress code, then have a dress code. But get to it. Say it simply and directly. And here's another thing you may want to think about. Allow for input, but keep yourself guided by the awareness of who needs to enforce the policy. If something comes out looking and sounding really silly, remember that you are the one who will have to bear the burden of ultimate enforcement. One of the great faculty tricks designed to make administrators look truly foolish is to force a silly policy that resolves little if anything important and then drop the stupid thing squarely in your lap. I doubt that this behavior is intentional; it just happens, and principals allow it. So stop.

One needs to have a good laugh over all the outrageous things that get written into policy as the collective knee jerk of the enforcement police. If all those who write policy have such a passion for the process, encourage them to seek public office as legislators; they'll have a field day immersed in policy. But never allow anyone to put a policy on the books that forces any staff member to look absurd. Here's one that was real: A foreign language teacher had a rule about underlining irregular verbs in red. One of her students just did not understand the rule about the red pencil. So after the third or fourth visit over the rule, she demanded that the principal call the young lad's father and inform him that his son was suspended for five days. The principal asked the fine teacher what reaction she thought the dad, a chief of surgery in a major university medical school, might have. Here's the discussion: "Dr. Smith, I am suspending your son for five days because he does not have a red pencil." Sound nuts? You bet it does. It has nothing to do with support or the lack of support for the teacher or for a policy. It has a lot to do with not looking stupid.

I suppose it would be interesting to perform a sort of statistical workup of the time required to enforce school and district policies.

If we took, for example, the attendance policy and computed how much time was spent in making the policy work and enforcing the rules and dealing with the consequences, we might be laid low by the results. Talk about time wasting! Some teachers in your school may well be satisfied wasting other people's (read assistant principal's) time. So let's put some of the enforcement burden on the teachers. Better still, let's get rid of the policies and the rules that consume inordinate amounts of time. Then let's use the time saved for the purposeful activities of teaching.

As a point of discussion, call to mind some of the following:

- Attendance policies that never got anyone to come to school.
- Homework policies that were just slightly dumber than some of the actual homework assignments.
- Dress codes that never caused young people to look any less bizarre than they sometimes do. (By the way, the mandate to look bizarre comes from a greater deity than is found in the student handbook. Come on! Kids look bizarre—they're supposed to. And they often look quite good as they look bizarre. No policy or rule should say that kids need to look like adults. How boring that would be. Can you imagine how bad it would be if all of us were required to look like lawyers, or bankers, or chefs, or whatever? Thank goodness that kids have the creative sense to look weird. And it's all right. Their appearance will improve, or not, as they get older.)
- Tardy policies that create work for no one other than the assistant principal.
- Rules, policies, and regulations that require bands of lawyers to interpret. What could we do with the money that we spend for legal advice? We think we need the lawyers because no one understands the rules we write. Let's create a new annual award for the school district with the clearest rules requiring no legal interpretation.
- Policies that do little except consume resources. Think for a moment or two about all the legal battles you read about in School Law 101. Case law develops because of thoughtless mis-reading of policy. The principals and administrators use

resources because they make mistakes. The rules present the problems. Think about all the tort issues raised over zero tolerance; the cases were mostly resolved in favor of the school or the school board. But consider this: In most of the cases, the school or board ended up looking stupid. Second, the school or board used up lots of taxpayer dollars to define the validity of a silly suspension over the possession of a nail clipper.

We all know that there is mindlessness about policies that are designed to cover all the contingencies. The policies seldom deal with the truly important issues. An attendance policy should say, "Come to school." The exciting things that happen in classrooms all over the country should support the policy. If you want to write a good attendance policy, you somehow need to have a policy that suggests we get kids excited about what happens in the classroom. More often than not, children stay away from schools because they are frustrated with some of the mindless things that happen in their classrooms. They get upset dealing with adults who dislike students. Their attendance has very little to do with the impact of television, the music on MTV, or the distractions of video games.

16

Reward Success in Your School

One of the frustrations of anyone working in any organization is the sense that no one pays attention, that no one cares. This may be an overstatement. Yes, we all know that worker bees get their rewards in their paychecks. But we also know all the good organizational research about what keeps people happy and motivated. We really do know—even when we act as though we don't have a clue—that simple forms of recognition are as powerful as trophies, raises, and the more tangible and substantive "tokens" given out in organizations. One does not need to hold Employee Recognition Days; one never really has to do The Day of the Teacher. Think for a moment about all the corporate hotshots who are wending their way to jail cells. Lots of those guys were richly rewarded. But to what end? What is needed is an honest, trusting, and straightforward piece of simple reinforcement sending a clear "Thanks" message. Feedback, as Tom Peters pointed out, is truly the Breakfast of Champions.

Rewarding success in your school may amount to random acts of appreciation. Of course, no one ever really takes the time to talk to principals, new and experienced, about the ways of simple rewards. We are so freaked out these days by all the garbage associated with "high-stakes" testing that we forget to offer praise and reward for things that some consider "givens" in schools. The other great reward myth lies in the crazy notion that a principal should never offer a positive comment like "You did a great job involving the students in that discussion." The fear is that the comment might come back to haunt the principal. What? Are we completely nuts?

So much of what teachers and principals deal with these days is predicated on the notion that nothing they do will make any difference. Just listen to those who tout religious, political, or home school agendas. They insist there is no hope for public education. No way! If you listen to the chatter offered by Bill Bennett and by Chester Finn you might think that our schools are in desperate straits. On the contrary, there is nothing but hope and a bright shining future for public education. There are fewer dropouts these days than in previous years. We graduate a higher percentage of students from high school than we ever did. Not too bad. And all of it will get better when we all start paying attention to the things that deserve rewarding.

What follows are some thoughts about the way reward systems apply in all schools. Let's start with the students and what one needs to reward in their actions and behaviors:

- Start by acknowledging the students' getting to school. In so many instances it is outrageously difficult for many of them to get out of the house and through the streets safely to get to school. So thank the little loves for getting there looking so good (or bad). Another aside: Have you ever considered the miracles of getting thousands and thousands of little people to arrive at all those separate places at the same time on the same days? My goodness, now there's something wonderful!
- Every time you catch one of the students doing something good (even almost good), provide some acknowledgment, some verbal reinforcement, and some reward.
- Allow some of the marginal behaviors and activities to go unnoticed. Let some of it go. Never look the other way for a violation of a rule that supports safety and health in school. But you know you can nod a bit on the rules that have marginal consequences if broken. (Here's one: Write on only one side of

the paper.) Oh, by the way, find the section on rules, regulations, and policies. It's no wonder that most teachers forget to reward accomplishments. The principals have them so focused upon enforcing rules that they have little time for creative and loving responses. Consider this as well: The rules the teachers are required to maintain may not be so important anyway.

- Every day, give every child something that each of them can be good at, something where they can succeed. Now creating lessons and activities that guarantee students' success may demand lots of creativity from the teachers. Let's hear it for creativity. In *In Search of Excellence*, Tom Peters refers to this maneuver as small gains. Allow those in the organization to make small gains all the time. Then step back and watch the way things will go. And every time someone in your school makes a small gain, lay on the reinforcement and the praise. Praising and reinforcing are the ways of reward!

- Stop with the testing nonsense. It is impossible to reward children for anything that has to do with group, schoolwide, district, or state testing, particularly with the way these global testing programs are run and implemented. Group rewards are hard. Group accomplishment plays to the great median. Let's go after some individual pats on the back and get back to what teaching has always been about. Does anyone think that children take such pride in the fact that their entire grade did well? More to the point is the fact that kids want to know, "Hey, whadja get?" You must do the testing; we all know that. But soft-pedal the testing. Let yourself become the first test case! Stop the hype and all the weeks and weeks of dreadful preparatory activities. Focus on the rewards of learning the important lessons, the content that needs teaching. Once the students have mastered the discipline of learning, the test results will take care of themselves.

- We need not engage in devising and implementing artificial recognition programs. Rather, we need to teach teachers and principals to honor and respect all types of student achievement at all levels in school.

Now we need to turn our attention as principals to the teachers and to the staff.

- Provide a list of actions and behaviors that are always rewarded in your school. Is attendance a big deal? Then reward perfect monthly attendance or weekly attendance. Does punctuality count? Then make a big deal about being on time. Teachers are supposed to return papers. Teachers are supposed to be nice. Principals are supposed to be fair. And smart. Come on! Make the argument for what you expect, then reward the behavior every time you detect it.

- Make certain that every teacher in the school understands what rewarding anything is all about. Make no assumptions that an adult necessarily knows how to reward anything.

- Teach the staff about the look of reinforcement and about how reinforcement is done. Then when you as the principal catch someone on the staff rewarding things that count, acknowledge the teacher's behavior. Let that teacher know that you truly appreciate his or her reinforcing actions.

- List the behaviors in the teachers' repertoire that are rewarded in your school. Here's a partial list if you are having trouble responding right now. At our school, we reward:
  - Courteous behavior, one staff member to another
  - Actively supporting and living the school's vision
  - Attentive behavior at faculty and group meetings
  - Following the few policies and directives that are part of our school
  - Timeliness and promptness
  - Loving our students
  - Respecting moms and dads
  - Devoting ourselves to individual and collective responsibilities
  - Any other nice thing that you can think of

- An aside: As the principal, you need to be the perfect model for these behaviors. Never expect your teachers to do things you cannot do yourself.

- Discover tasks and assignments that your staff can do with remarkable success. Have them do those things. Reward them.

Most people know about the positive result achieved by rich and specific feedback. Most successful strategies of behavioral change and cognitive development lean heavily upon positive feedback, upon reward for accomplishment. But the fashion these days is to beat up educators. Why? Maybe teachers and principals are easy targets who lack a strong lobby to care for them. Most of the teachers' associations lack focus to deal with issues that pertain to greatness. Certainly, the principals' associations have some sort of agenda that has wandered away from strong advocacy for excellent performance.

The smart people who speak for the principals and for the teachers need to return to the basics. The basics have to do with direct and specific ways of extolling the hard work that their members do. That is a strong agenda that will show the professional organizations as true and real advocates. Too often the public relations viewpoint is that the organizations need to convey a balanced view. No, they don't. The professional organizations need to become very blatant in their protection of their rank and file. The principals' and teachers' organizations absolutely must extol what their members do. No one else will. End of rant.

Let's have a resounding return to advocacy. If there are no others who can muster the energy to extol the achievements of principals and teachers, then principals and teachers need to make their own advocacy noises. They should reward with their votes and with their membership fees only those individuals, groups, and politicians who take their side in recognizing the significant work they accomplish in the schools. If you cannot be on our side and if you cannot support what is good for us, we cannot support you. This simplistic perspective is obvious: If you cannot be part of the solution, you are probably part of the problem. Simplistic, no doubt. But here the simplicity of strong advocacy is required and needed.

Here are some reasonable strategies to support rewarding what you and your school do:

• Always have specific and accurate information for everyone touched by the organization. Never be put off by the fact that others may not use what you give them. Provide the data and information anyway so that those disposed to brag about you will have the information they need.

- Make contributions (financial) to only those political candidates who speak positively about teachers and principals.
- Join the campaigns of those candidates who take an active role in supporting education and rewarding the hard work educators do.
- Write critical letters to any politician who speaks negatively about education and about educators. You need not be nasty or surly. You do need to be direct. You also need to be informed and accurate. Too often the adversaries lack an informed and accurate view. Finally, you need to be prepared to get into a bit of trouble.
- Whenever the media in your community make disparaging remarks about what goes on in your school, persuade your staff to write strong responses to the TV station, the radio station, or the newspaper. Respond with your checkbook or your cash. Stop patronizing those who advertise in the local media.
- Keep the politicians in the community (that includes your own board) richly informed about what happens in your school. Then ask all of them to use the information you provide to support what you and your people do. Seek the support at budget time. Give the board and the local politicians a really good occasion to demonstrate their support.
- Learn to say, "I have no comment about that" when someone seeks to get you to say awful and negative things about schools, about your boss, about your colleagues, or about education.
- When a colleague, supervisor, or board member makes up information rather than use the accurate information you provide, ask them why they fabricate or provide inaccurate information.

17

Spend Time with Students

Get out of the office and get into the classroom, the gym, the cafe, the auditorium, and out on the playing field. Be where the students are. There is something quite significant about the presence of The Great One in the midst of the things that happen day to day in schools. My sense is that students in schools like the principal, particularly when the principal acts as though he or she enjoys students and likes being around them. Students like individuals who are sensitive to their needs and aware of their faults and problems, who treat them with regard and respect, and who consistently enforce what needs enforcing. They take pride in sharing their one story about the prom, the cafeteria, the study hall, the after-game party, and about the way the principal interacted and reacted to what students said and did. Part of the significant history of the school gets wrapped around the students' memories and impressions of the principal's role in those happenings.

Students recognize and respond to loving adults. Now do not get all crazy over the words "loving adults." Too many models of principals' skills and behaviors are built upon the most distorted examples of the old jock and the retired military person. (As an aside, why do some decision makers think that veteran colonels and lieutenant colonels will make good principals? What is there in the background of these soldiers that signals "effective principal"? If their resumes show good hard productive work in schools, then give them a chance to lead a school. Some superintendents might be a little too willing to hand over a school to the soldier types. Someone in charge needs to get all these "by the numbers" and "by the book" individuals retooled for other things.)

Back to the loving adult concept. Look around your school. Do you see any evidence of strong, compassionate, loving leadership? If the answer is "no" or "not really," then that role as loving and compassionate adult is open to you as principal. You really need not be a strident martinet of a leader who beats on people and takes names. There is too much of that metaphor that resounds in schools. You need to take charge of compassionate leadership for your students. The young ones need to be loved and respected. Once you get that right, you can coast toward achievement. If they love you, love the school, love the teachers, then all the bad stuff goes out the window. The students will take to the tasks of achieving. How do I know that? I just know it. The data on high-performing organizations (schools and other places requiring leadership) contain some startling and interesting visions of achievement in the presence of love and compassion. And all that results from being with the students.

The principal needs to make the decision that the greater part of his or her day belongs to the kids. That means getting into the places where the kids are. You know kids spend lots of time in classroom; show up there. Let the kids know you have an active interest in teaching and learning, and then you will definitely fill the role of instructional leader. And you will send such a strong message to the students. That message will take hold and they will know what they mean to you because you spend time with them and not with all the silly things that seem to plague a principal. Ask your students about how they are doing in class. Talk to them about learning. Use language that emphasizes intellectual achievement. Use that language with all the students, not just the honors students. When all the children hear you talk to them and with them about what they are doing in the classroom and what they do with their homework, you and they are joined in an enriching purpose. In a very substantial way, you are participating in cooperative learning at the highest level.

Here are some actions and behaviors for your consideration:

- Greet students every morning with a comment about their homework assignments from the night before. You might also give the ones you greet some nice compliment.

- Get into the corridors during the passing periods. Smile. Talk pleasantly with the staff and with the students. Let the assistant principal and the department chairs check the bathrooms and other places where some of the bad guys lurk.

- Every day, talk with the students and address each of them by name. Learn a new name or two each day.

- Seek out the students who have done something swell on a given day. Go find them and lay it on them. Let them know how happy you are with what they have done.

- Never, never walk away from something nasty going on in your school. Correct with directness and with passion. Let the young charges understand that you love them but dislike intently the awful thing you just saw them do. It is the action, not the actor, that gets corrected.

- Catch them doing something good. Reinforce the good behavior. Tell them in rich language what a joy it is to see them behaving the way they are.

- Talk to your staff about honoring the presence of the students in the school. Shift the conversations from what bad kids we have to how lucky we are to have the kids we have.

- Refuse to tolerate anything in your school that demeans the students and the teachers. I have addressed all that in other parts of this book.

- Let the students see you lots and lots. Be everywhere. Put specific times and places on your calendar and show up. Make certain that the greater portion of your day belongs to the students and the staff.

- Be there as the students leave for the day. Let your face be the first they see when they arrive and the last they see when they leave. And make sure yours is smiling.

18

Understand the Nonrational

Here's a rule that often seems not to work: If we put our best effort into this, everything will be all right. Sounds like a rather reasonable statement. Under most circumstances this rule applies. However, as an organizational principle, it is so often very wrong. Much good effort has been steadfastly put into issues and tasks that have gone completely and irretrievably down the drain. More often than not, we simply do not understand what has gone wrong even when we have applied logic and best effort. Sometimes all the logic of hard work and right answers proves to be really quite ineffective.

Let's face it, if progress were marked by solid effort, by dedicated and committed effort, then we would be immersed in smashing successes all the time. But what is the condition we face? Pretty bad. And no one can be blamed for making lots of rational efforts that are based on pretty reasonable thinking and planning. Most of the innovation, most of the revisions, most of the interesting things we do and talk about have all been based upon large doses of rational effort, rational research, logic, and solid attempts. And many times so much of our efforts are not worth diddly. Why? Who knows? Blame Murphy! Blame the off-kilter disposition and alignment of the planets. But the sad fact is that even the best developed and the most judiciously deployed plans go belly up.

Most of the planners, the thinkers, the writers, the researchers, and certainly most of the pundits think the answers are embedded in rational approaches to things. Not a chance. We'd better make some adjustments to our logic compasses. Go get a copy of that famous poem by Robert Burns; you know, the one that addresses the "best laid plans of mice and men. . . ."

The answer to all this lies in a mischievous inclination to trust the nonrational, the bit of serendipity that overtakes us every now and then. You and I know there is not always a reasonable response to what works and what does not work. We know that some of the stuff with which we deal might possibly hinge on the phases of the moon. Yet we grope with policy and procedure and minutes and meetings, thinking that all the answers lie somewhere in that cave of logic. We need to trust the imp in us. Why do we admit with a twinkle in the eye that, "Yes, things seem different when there is a full moon"?

There may be no answers for many of the questions that boards and research groups and committees and self-appointed seekers after truth ask you. How often has a principal been confronted with a question like this: "Why are the recent test scores lower?" Or how about this one: "Why doesn't every student have a textbook?" Here's another one: "I thought all the computers were to be delivered last week. What happened?" Watch the poor principal struggle to discover some logical answer that sounds more intelligent than "The teamsters were on strike" or "The truck broke down." Also, get ready for the interesting context for the embarrassing questions. The interrogator never asks the question in private; he or she puts the question to you in a setting conducive to maximum damage.

Let's consider some of the following:

- We work really hard to determine what path we might take to increase test scores in any given subject. We plead with the board to allocate funds to create a committee composed of bright, hard-working, and dedicated teachers. We charge a zealous committee chair with well-defined tasks. We may even set aside funds to pilot the results of the committee's hard work. What happens is that the recommendations fail to happen. It was all sound effort driven by good people whose intentions were beyond question. But the program just did not work.

- Too many of the students are late for class. They meander through the halls after the bell, and they arrive late for class. Enough of that, we state firmly. So we gather the best faculty to devise a new tardy policy that covers all the contingencies of tardy behavior. The efforts receive a round of applause. The condition continues to deteriorate. The kids are still late. And someone is stuck with the burdensome task of enforcing a new set of rules that just do not make things happen the way they might.

- As the principal you have worked really hard preparing a very specific and nonrefutable budget with logical and cogent backup. You have your PowerPoint presentation and handouts ready to fly. Your time has come and you are so well prepared that there is minimal margin for error. Your presentation is marvelous, well received, and smiled over to a fare-thee-well. But your budget is rejected.

What? How can this happen? Well, the imp of the nonrational has rushed into the fray and has stolen someone's thunder and logic. Something has misfired. When you examine the logical and the rational work that went into your effort, you miscalculated one thing—sometimes logic matters little. There is nothing you can do about that except regroup and lick your wounds.

As a principal you need to know the nonrational and be prepared to deal with the consequences. Give some of the following observations a moment's consideration:

- Sometimes experienced staff act as though they have just arrived in the building.

- Even when your written directive is as clear as it can be, someone will ask, "What do you mean by this?"

- Not everyone on the staff reads the memos and the policy manual.

- Even when they read what you want them to read, some of the staff interpret the written word in their subjective way. Then they probably wander around asking their colleagues, "What do you think she meant by this?"

- Every now and then someone will drive into school using the exit route.
- After all the in-service work you do about coding attendance forms and records, one of your staff will devise a new coding system. That person likes his better than yours.
- Maybe you have noticed that some staff members never leave the building promptly when the fire evacuation bell rings.
- I suspect that everyone in your building understands that school starts at 7:45 A.M.

You could probably add many, many things to this list of nonrational events in your organization. Probably I am overstating it when I suggest that the nonrational makes absolutely no sense. Neither does having thousands of students in one building make sense. Neither does taking two instructional days away from students to test their eyes. Neither does spending day after day focused upon the state testing program. Neither does cropping a day each week off the schedule because some other department in the city or town government has run out of money. But it is what it is. You as the principal must learn to tolerate and anticipate the nonrational and be prepared to deal with nonrational events in a rational way.

So we might revisit some of the things we have been talking about.

- Have good plans in place.
- Even if your good plan looks great, have a backup, a B plan, and a C plan.
- Make things as simple as they can be.
- Refuse to allow others to complicate your organization.
- Develop an appreciation for the kind of stuff that happens the day before a holiday or during the first snowfall.
- Keep talking about your expectations for the behavior of others.
- Use lots of repetitions.
- Understand the peculiarities of the Delphi system. You are correct in knowing that N heads are better than one, but those heads need to be screwed on tightly.

- Value redundant systems.
- Prevent others (read assistant superintendents, district directors) from imposing some procedure on your school that you know will undoubtedly result in nonrational consequences.

We are not guaranteeing that any of these things will work. We suggest, however, considering these steps might prove engaging and fruitful enough so the guys from the funny farm never show up at your office door with a big net to use to drag you away.

19

Talk About Your Own Success

Now is the time for building the image of the leader. Never mind all the talk about the Peter Principle. Most of the administrators we know got jobs simply because someone in the organization thought the appointed, selected, designated individual could get things done, and most have a story to tell. Each individual who moves into the principal's office or the vice-principal's office got there by dint of his or her track record. And several of them were never coaches (coaching may not be such a bad career track, by the way).

Despite our inclination to believe it, people are not appointed to positions of leadership because they are the lowest bidders. And they are not anointed and appointed because they have "connections." Nor are they made principals because they were the only candidates. They receive their appointments because someone in the community served by the school believes that the appointed person can actually get the job done. By the way, there may be several in your school who were supporting another choice for principal. They already think you are inept and have been selected incorrectly. They may or may not like you. Their feelings have little or maybe nothing to do with your qualifications—they think that someone else deserved the job you got.

It has become fashionable to adopt a cynical view of all this interview and appointment stuff. If the truth be told, more often than not the one getting the job is the most talented and the most suited to perform well. But maybe not the most well liked or popular, at least not with the locals.

We get so overwhelmed with the cynical view that we become numbed to the reality that bright people get jobs as principals. Here's a word or two for those who get the jobs: In a quiet and direct way, state your case. Pronounce your mission and move along toward success. Make no apologies because you got the job. Avoid silly and shallow apologies for your success. "Oh, yes. The board gave me the job because they wanted to clean things up." What is that all about? These custodial metaphors really serve no purpose. "I got the job because they wanted someone who had a curriculum background." What? Try this one: "I got the job because I was the most qualified. Thank you for asking. Oh, and thanks for your support." Stop talking and get into the batter's box.

Make a list of the things that got you where you are right now. Take your time. List the things that make you proud to be a principal or the candidate for the next principal's opening, things that you do, things that define your successes. I am not talking about a list of hollow or shallow boasts. I am talking about the things that make you the professional that you are. Now after you have exhausted yourself with all your notes on the list, reexamine that list with rightful pride. How does it look? Do you feel a sense of accomplishment? Would your mom be pleased? Does your family feel good about what you have done? If you answer "yes" to these questions and if you now have a smile on your face because you feel good, then never, never apologize for your accomplishments. Quit feeling as though the appointment is a matter of luck. You got the job because you are good.

Now that you have the job, take some time to outfit your office with the things that remind you of your successes and accomplishments. You do know that the visitors to your office will examine your office the same way those visitors look for the doctor's credentials when they report for a physical examination.

Doctors frame and hang their certificates and diplomas because those pieces of paper announce degrees of qualification. So never deny your accomplishments by refusing to hang your awards, certificates, diplomas, and letters of accomplishments and thanks in conspicuous places in your office. All those "artifacts" announce who you are and what you are. They are forms of pedigree. Despite our current politically correct views that one should never be better than another (gag), you need to extol your own successes to let those around you know that you are not some jerk who stumbled into the position of leadership simply because someone inadvertently left the door ajar.

Understand your own strengths and skills. When you plan well and take the time to think the problem through, you have applied your best talents and efforts. You need to acknowledge your gifts and be willing to talk quietly about how hard you work and about how skilled you are. There is nothing wrong with that. Know yourself, as the saying goes. It strikes me as peculiar that so many people talk about enhancing one's self-image. Why are talented principals left out of the mix of those seeking to establish a positive self-image? Does not a leader need support in building a self-image? There exists a contradictory perspective that one should be capable to achieve the success that is the principalship but at the same time should never tout the abilities that are part of the job.

that have far-reaching implications. To decide if a student can or cannot do a particular thing may not have wide-reaching implications, despite what we think about consistency.

By the way, where did we ever get so hung up on the need to be consistent in responding to requests? I don't get it! We keep arguing that what we do for one we need to do for all. New rule: What you do for one, you do for one. You take each issue on a case-by-case basis. If you are criticized for inconsistency, so what? And if you are criticized for favoritism, so what! Don't we and they (whoever they are) sound like babies? In responding to needs, our responses and reactions may appear tinged by favoritism. But we are trying to get things done, to resolve issues. That's exactly what principals do. They get things resolved; they make things happen. They move items off the to-do list. So the school leader who moves to resolve issues must favor his or her students and teachers above all others. We favor our defined mission and purposes above anything else. That form of favoritism strengthens our resolve to get things done.

One accomplishes things by doing. Not by holding meetings; not by formulating more unneeded policy. We sure have enough of that. And who ever said that boards of education are empowered to make decisions that are better made closer to the root cause, the root issue, or the root problem? Why should boards make decisions about whether kids go on field trips or not? About whether the buses come earlier today or later? Why does any board or any superintendent feel the need to ponder the way lunch is handled in your school? Why is it that so many people have such an overwhelming need to make decisions about what goes on in your school, particularly when it comes to defining the basic school rules and regulations? We probably have too many boards, board members, rules, policies, regulations, and committees, all distracted by things that seldom serve the school's vision. So much of all that protocol stuff really gets in the way of making decisions and getting things done. It may serve the vision when a principal says "no" to the question "Does the board know anything about this?" Some things need never be brought to the board.

Yes, we know that principals sometimes take too much time trying to figure out what a staff member or a student wants to do. Maybe some of our colleagues become overwhelmed and reasonably dimwitted. Here's what we mean: A teacher comes to the principal or the assistant principal and says that the copy machine is not working. Too often the administrator asks, "What do you mean, the copy machine is not working?" There's a probing and insightful question. Why does the administrator need to interrogate the staff member? Well, you say, you never know if the teacher just didn't know how to work the machine. Get serious. You are hoping that the teacher can help raise test scores and you question his or her ability to know if a machine works. Your response is to say, "I will get someone on it right away." Go get someone to fix it now and forget the questions that insult you and the teacher. Give the staff member the name of the one who does fix it, or go fix it yourself. Just stop wasting time with go-nowhere responses.

"We have run out of paper." Quit trying to determine whose fault that is; just get some paper. And stop giving mini lectures about budget expenditures. No one really cares! "The kids have messed up the first-floor lavatory." Now, here's a chance to convene the discipline committee. Wrong. Find the custodian and get it cleaned up. By the way, do not discuss the lack of respect indicated by the messy lavatory; the mess in the lavatory will continue to ruin somebody's day. The custodian's job is to take care of the problem needing his or her attention. Done. Do it. That's all. You might say to the custodian, "I understand your frustration, and I am sorry for this. But now you need to go to the lavatory and clean up the mess. Thank you very much." You need no policy for that. You need not waste time talking with a union steward. You simply need to take care of the problem. Don't you love action-oriented behavior?

Here is something that we know for certain: when immediate issues are handled, there may be little reason for anyone to yammer about the principal's apparent lack of concern. In fact, when the little issues and problems are handled, they usually fail to become big issues. It works like this: There are broken windows. You fail to get the windows repaired. Now you have two problems—the broken windows and your apparent lack of concern. Never mind the custodian and the work orders. Just get the bloody windows repaired even if you have to call the hardware store and pay for the repair out of your pocket. Never mind that the head custodian or the chief of maintenance complains. Your response needs to be simply that the windows will be repaired one way or the other—immediately. If that bothers the hierarchy, then so be it. If they complain, tell them the complaints will stop once the repairs are made. Or as someone once said, the hangings will stop once the guilty parties are discovered.

Quit caring about the embarrassment brought upon the heads of the incompetent. If you really worry about inappropriate reactions, buy the custodial staff coffee and sit down with them to tell them what you expect. Those around you need to respond positively or they need to get out. That reinforces the need for immediate reaction. Think of all this as a form of triage. What needs to be done quickly gets done. What can wait, well, we will give it some time. Now after that entire harangue about moving quickly, let me provide this one caution. Please, please make certain that you are not a quick gun with decisions that have far-reaching consequences.

Consider this before we leave this section: If you are certain that the simple request to leave school grounds places the student asking permission in jeopardy, then say "No." If you know that the staff member asking for permission to run home will get there and back with no problems, then say "Yes." Do you remember the notion of unanticipated consequences? If you think clearly that you have factored in the unanticipated stuff, then move along. You need to trust things like the petitioner's track record and your intuition, gut feeling, and good sense. But you need not convene a committee, seek wide-ranging input, or take a survey. You need to act.

22

Take Some Time for Yourself

Somehow there is a truth to this observation: The health of the organization is directly related to the health of the leader of that organization. Ummm. Sounds reasonable. What this means is that when the leader acts in dysfunctional and inappropriate ways (translate as *crazy*), then the rest of the organization gets weird. One can almost sense the nuttiness as one enters a school where the leader does not exercise reasonable control over self. Anyone who has even the slightest familiarity with schools and with the business of schools knows well that there are times when it is really difficult to keep everything under control. An effective job description, however, should have this statement as part of it: "Maintains effective control over one's life—intellectual, spiritual, emotional, and physical—most of the time."

One of the best ways to keep things moving along in the right direction and in keeping with the vision is to maintain a strong sense of well-being. And well-being derives from taking care of oneself. Stay well. Keep yourself strong in mind and body. Go smell the flowers and the coffee. When it's time for a vacation, take it. One must certainly get tired of listening to those who exclaim that they are the first one in the building and the last one out each day. Wow! That's really impressive. Maybe we should ask that person if he or she has a custodian in the building who might get things opened up and shut down. What's really impressive is not how early or how late one is around. Rather, what impresses most is the effectiveness of the behavior while on the scene. Healthy people behave in healthy and effective ways. That's it! One way to stay healthy is to take time for personal and professional needs.

Give some of the following pointers a thought or two. Take to heart the ones that make sense to you. Run by the ones that really do not speak to you or your needs.

- Take the needed time for your physical well-being. Exercise in ways that are good for you. Get into a program, join the Y, work out in your own gym. Get some help and support from a member of your PE staff.

- Spend time with your family. Take the time to linger over a cup of coffee with your spouse. Every now and then take your spouse for a nice quiet walk where people will not be greeting you and telling you about how you need to run the school. Visit with your own kids over breakfast. By the way, this means that you require your family members to be sane on those mornings.

- Take some time for a hobby that makes you feel good. Who cares what that hobby is? Just do something that distracts you from the activities that are very much a part of your job and the work demands.

- Do something spiritual now and again. I am not talking about some big spiritual routine. All that is wonderful, of course. Rather, I am talking about a stop at the local church you attend for a moment or two of quiet. I am referring to a few minutes of spiritual reading of some sort. You see, our lives rest on the tripod of the physical, intellectual, and spiritual activities reflecting who and what we are. So take time for each of these pieces of your life.

- Plan the time for the necessary physical examinations in your life. Visit your doctor once a year. Get your teeth checked. Report for your annual eye examination. Preventive personal care and maintenance is really good.

- Find some ways to recharge your batteries. When I talk about yoga and massage and some of the "new age" things, most of my principal friends think I have grown weird. But more and more, people understand just how effective these activities are. Think about some of the holistic parts of your life, and quit thinking that you will show weakness if you acknowledge the need for meditation or for some form of Zen relief.

- Every now and then, actually take some quiet time in your own building and office. And never, ever tell me that you just cannot do that. Pardon me, are you not in charge? Where in your job description does it say that you must be engaged *all* the time? Do you really feel it necessary to be always on deck, always responding?

23

Stay Intellectually Challenged

Atrophy is the natural tendency of living things to run down if they go unchallenged. Things run down; if they do not run down, they slow down. The human intellect demands challenge to keep it stimulated. Most schools certainly provide lots of challenge. But I am not sure that the challenges a principal faces each day necessarily stimulate the higher cognitive centers of the brain. The research on aging (all of us do that, by the way) points to the need for constant intellectual stimulation as a way to keep us from getting stale, forgetful, and slightly nuts.

So what things do you do to sustain intellectual challenge? Allow me to pose a few questions and to make some statements for your consideration. You might want to grab your journal to record some of your own responses. By the way, keeping a journal is a neat way to engage in intellectual stimulation. So here goes:

- Do you presently do things that are purely intellectual? Do you know what your intellectual strengths and weaknesses are?
- Do you have a specifically defined professional development program? Does your professional development program build upon your recognized and identified strengths and developmental needs?

- Have you enlisted the support of a mentor to assist you in carrying out each of the components of your developmental plan?
- Do you set aside some time each day for personal reading?
- What do you read? Take a piece of paper and write down the three or four books that you have read recently. Nothing comes to mind? Therein lies the point of this little inquiry.
- In your journal, write down the titles of five or six classics of literature you wish you had read. Make a plan to acquire those great books. Set aside about twenty minutes each day and read.
- Do you send handwritten notes and letters to your friends and family? Actually, communicating this way is really a nice intellectual stimulus. Writing with a pen stimulates both cognitive and motor skills. (I stress ink pen here. Go out and buy yourself a nice pen. More on that later.) One or two of the experts on writing tell us that writing is a great way of thinking one's way into a subject.
- Buy some nice writing paper and a fine writing instrument (an ink pen). A friend of mine owns a very high quality ink pen, a really expensive one. He told me in conversation one day that he uses a felt tip pen for jotting notes, for making the grocery list. He uses his fine ink pen for writing and composing. That is an interesting distinction.
- Do you take the time to visit art museums? First, it's a great outing made more enjoyable if you take your family. Kids love art museums and galleries. They are fascinated by the colors and the forms, and you will be too. You seldom meet people there who want to tell you how to do your job. Get a guidebook; rent the audiotapes that provide the tour and the commentary about what you are viewing; take a nice intellectually stimulating walk. But, you ask, "What does this have to do with my job?" Everything. After several months of once-in-a-while visits you will definitely notice a difference in your perceptions of the realities of your job.
- Do you ever wish you could speak another language? Those in the know tell us that language acquisition is a great form of

mental workout. Why not visit your Spanish classes often? See how the sounds and the forms of another language stimulate. Buy some language tapes. Take a few minutes each day and exercise your brain.

- Do the adults in your building get together for things like "reading groups"? Try it. Lead them. Buy the books for the group out of the staff development funds.
- Do you enjoy listening to music? What's your choice? You know that there is such a thing as the Mozart Effect, which suggests that certain mental skills are enhanced by listening to Wolfgang's music. Researchers have done some interesting work on the suggestion that classical and baroque music tune up the brain. So go jack up the volume and get smart.
- At some point, get a copy of *How to Think Like Leonardo DaVinci* by Michael Gelb. This one book may well open up some interesting possibilities that will intellectually improve your leadership patterns and behaviors. You may also look for books by effective CEOs. But be careful with some of the current "hero mythology." All these execs write their own stuff, and sometimes it is a bit hyperbolic.

Maybe you have forgotten that the initial qualifications for the principal's job rested more squarely on what you knew, rather than on what you did. Think for a moment about the intellectual challenge required to slog through those umpteen credits to complete the advanced degree work. Getting the degree put you in the talent pool. You probably came across the way you did in your interview because you sounded reasonably bright. I believe that. Your mental skills stood you well in the process of becoming famous.

Now that you have the job, you must, you absolutely must do all you can do to maintain the edge, the intellectual sharpness, to keep you out in front. You will be challenged daily to display your intellectual edge. The intellectually unchallenged leaders are very quickly found out and the consequences of that discovery are rather severe. Your intellectual challenges lie not in your ability to prepare the master schedule or to figure out the budget. My goodness, almost anyone can learn all that nonsense. The challenge is to understand the analogs of leadership in Caesar's *Commentaries*, or in Henry V's speech to his men just before the Battle of Agincourt, or in Shackleton's challenge to get all of his comrades back to civilization. If you know anything about Winston Churchill's life, you may well understand the uses of intellectual challenge and stimulation. Oh, in case you forget, intellectual challenge and stimulation are the most significant issues that drive schools to success.

24

Share Information the Organization Needs

Few question that information is power. Some leaders, some principals, some teachers, in fact lots of people who have never thought about this behave as though all the data they hold onto makes them a bit more powerful. True! True!

So . . . here's the deal. You need to share the appropriate information you hold and have access to with the members of the organization. When you share the information, when you pass along the data, you make those around you as smart and as informed as you are. Information sharing may be one of the best empowering and collegial actions a principal can perform. When you pass the data around, all those who are touched by it and share it and pass it along are made a bit better by the information and by the act of sharing it. What happens, coincidentally, is that no one thinks you are trying to deny them access to anything that affects the organization.

Lots of negative things happen in schools where the uninformed think that the informed are hatching a plot, a cabal. Some staff members may always suspect hidden agendas designed to keep the unknowing in the dark. Thus, when members of the organization think the leader is trying to hide information, the gossip begins. The gossip cycle assumes a life force that drives it toward weird conclusions. Others who suspect a plot try like mad to be "in the know." When those "out of the loop" (I like that expression) are frustrated in their need to grab the news, they fabricate information. They counter the lack of information with some creative information hatched out of frustration. The efforts to get a piece of the information ratchets up the gossip, the stories, and the fabrications to a level that looks almost like truth.

Have you ever considered how unflattering and false stories start, grow, and become gossipy accusations that stick to the leader? The negative results and consequences flow from the "hidden agenda" and from the inability of the leader to confront the subtle stretches of the truth that turn into lies. The rule then should be "We keep nothing hidden from the staff." You may need to remind them that you are unable to share personnel information. But they may already have more information about colleagues than you do. So put as much information as you can out there for all to see and know.

Here are some topics that require lots of information from you. These are pieces of information that will keep everyone informed. You may add to the list, but this list may well be a good place to begin thinking about all you might share with your faculty. Just remind yourself that your teachers are entrusted with dozens of young minds and hearts; they really can handle the news. The ability and skills required to receive the information and to treat that information appropriately are acquired skills. These skills develop with practice. Give them the news; let them practice.

- Tell them how the budget is built; let them know where the money goes.
- Be honest with the staff about the things that you will ask for in the budget.
- As much as possible, let the staff share in the budget-making process; then keep them informed.
- Make certain they know that most salary information is a matter of public record. Tell the staff where that public record is located.
- Talk to the staff about new hires. Let them all know what you are looking for next year and let them know why you are seeking those positions.

- Be extra careful about the procedures for assigning staff to tasks for which they can make extra money. Let everyone in on how one gets those assignments.
- Inform the staff about how perks are doled out. If someone gets an extra special parking space, tell the faculty how that happened.
- Provide rich oral and written materials that are filled with information and data.
- Hold the staff responsible for reading the things that you distribute to them. Do not characterize the published material from your office as trivial or unimportant. And if it is, then do not, under any circumstances, send it out or waste time talking about it.
- Learn how to answer inquiries simply and specifically. Never hesitate to answer a question with an answer that looks like "Because that's what I determined we should do." Here's another unusual response: "Sorry. I can't answer that. I just don't know."

Waste no one's time with useless data. Try these questions as criteria you might use to decide what you will and will not share:

- Will this information make the staff and the kids and the school better for having it? Will someone be smarter? Better informed?
- Does sharing any of this violate any trust, any confidence, or any negotiated agreements?
- Have I presented the information in the simplest manner?
- Is this information truthful?
- Will the information lessen a problem?
- Will the least-informed member of my organization understand what this data is all about?
- Is there a strong possibility that my staff can convey this information accurately to people served by the school?
- What will happen if I simply keep quiet about all this?
- Is there anything contained here that sounds like half-truth or gossip?
- Is this information designed with mean-spirited ends in mind?
- Does this information enhance my staff with the sharing?
- Have I made a clear distinction between my opinions and the truth?

I guess most agree that information is power. One of the ironies of the empowerment movement is that too little information is shared to create empowered staff. The more necessary information the staff possesses, the better decisions they will make and the more autonomous they will act. So rich information flow may do the trick in moving your school, its mission, its goals, and its vision in the right direction. If you are trying to keep the craziness of large organizations to a minimum, you need to engage in truly empowering transactional behavior. Information sharing is a rich empowering behavior. So share what you know with the staff. Effective information sharing will really make some awful things go away.

25

Address Small Problems Early

How's that for classic Machiavelli? He was big on taking care of the small issues right away. Addressing issues and problems before they get too big makes sense. How often have really bright people said, "Oh, let it go; they'll act like the professionals they are"? Or, "No big deal; it will pass." Bad move, on the whole. Part of your professional behavior is contained in an assertive response to screw-ups, no matter how small, in your organization. When the mistakes are little, then you need to do little to address them. But you must address the small issues. Actually, you need little more than a direct word, spoken in a nice way that conveys strongly, "I do not like what you have done. Let me tell you specifically what you need to do to fix it." Simple words spoken early save lots of time and energy later on. Those simple words must be specific. Rather than say, "You need to take care of business," you need to say, "Return the papers within three days. Do not let the students wait three weeks."

Never rely on the implied threat of an evaluation process to get people to shape up. You know that we have been evaluating people for a long time. Most of the data suggests that all forms of evaluation rarely change problem behavior. Only relentless feedback and positive developmental intervention produce needed changes in behavior. Relentless feedback should have the look of strong

the principal dedicate your daily activities to taking care of the little things, your staff may be well protected against overload. Look, the teachers have a lot to deal with. You may go around all day thinking that no one has it harder than you. Oh, yes they do. At least you can hide out in your office for brief periods of time; you can grab a coffee or simply sit still. They cannot. So they need someone to buffer the problems for them. Get to the small things and get rid of them. Take care of the staff that way.

26

Keep Things Simple

Reading the policy handbooks and regulations developed, written, and presented by educators shows even the most confused individual that many educators refuse to pass up any chance to make the simple complex. A demon gets into the brain of an educator, and he or she makes things as obtuse as possible. If you do not get the gist of that, then grab the most available copy of a policy manual and read. It's probably enough to make you just slightly dazed and confused. Pick a topic, any topic. Is there an attendance policy that is really clear, simple, and direct? Any good attendance policy might read "Come to school." Or how about "The law says that you must come to school." But why should anything be that simple? A rule stated so directly implies the writer was not educated enough to be sufficiently obtuse. Mark Twain pointed out that all the degrees possessed by an individual suggest the individual was educated beyond his or her ability to deal with things. Was he talking about educators? Sometimes one may be suspicious of the efficacy of the degrees.

Of course, if you as a principal really want to support and foster confusion, then form a committee and have that gang write a policy. You might want to try a simple experiment. Gather up your most obsessive-compulsive staff members and ask them to write a tardy policy for the faculty. Now there's something that might get the blood stirred and the mind more boggled than it is. Here's a bet—the policy will be so "out there" that you will need some really smart staff to understand and interpret it. If you want to have lots of fun, get the staff to write a policy that says something about the acceptable length of young women's skirts. Or you might want to try the latest issue—bare midriffs at the prom. Go for it!

Often, when a principal takes on a new job, he or she takes on the task of revising existing policies. The existing policies written by less informed or less insightful predecessors seem not to fit the leadership the new principal brings to his or her assignment. What some new principals fail to understand is that the very policies they are playing around with were written by the staff who have been in the building longer than they have. These rules needing attention and revision may well represent the best efforts of lots of staff. So here we go changing the rules and insulting the staff who wrote them. Just leave those rules alone until you figure out what needs doing.

One of the larger corporations has an advertisement that suggests we need to keep it simple. One would never discern an inclination toward the simple in so many things that are part of school. The rule statements and the rule language get awfully befuddling. So the plea here is for revisions that simplify things.

Get out the student handbook and, even before you read it, resolve that you will shorten it by twenty-five percent. Right. You will work to get rid of needless content, not simply revise, rewrite, or edit. Rather you will eliminate; you will purge. My bet is that nothing and no one will be the worse for your cutting. Once you have the size of the rule book or policy manual squared away, you can devote some attention to the content and to the wording of the documents that confound.

Anticipate Confusion

Whoever said that schools are rational places? Those left-brained crazy people who adore sequence and order keep telling us that schools are serious, formal, and rational places. Wrong! There really is nothing rational about schools. I mean, come on, teaching anyone about the mysteries of decoding and language requires an almost absolute abandonment of logic and reason. It is preposterous to assume that we can teach the truths of our culture and our history to children. We also go along teaching some pretty complex and abstract information. We believe we can do all that, so we proceed. And we often fail to recognize just what confusion we create in the wake of all that learning. Anyone clutching this book has probably heard the voice of despair say, "I don't get it." I cannot imagine a teacher who has never listened to a young learner say in mild desperation, "I'm totally confused."

So we need special skills to anticipate all that continues to confuse and to go wrong in schools. I am talking about what takes place when we group large cohorts under one roof on even the best of days and expect all to go well. I am not talking about the deliberate efforts of some people to do mean and nasty things. There may be little accounting for those who refuse to follow directions, who never seem to get the policies right, or who just plain ignore their responsibilities. All that creates confusion enough. There it is: the marginal chaos that is part of large organizations, all the confusion that can never be mitigated or lessened by handbooks or policies or regulations. Further, you may be unable to write rules to get anything to line up. God created teenagers as a supremely confusing test for adults. The lack of alignment creates chaos and confusion. We become marginally crazy thinking that firm rules and policies will make all the confusion go away. It all defies logic, but it is a great challenge.

Good rules and positive enforcement of the rules will make things work . . . to a point. Then nature, or the confluence of the planets, or the phases of the moon, or something takes over and sets our teeth on edge. Obviously staff members are failing to do the job because the job seems so exasperating in some of its complexities. The job just becomes overwhelming; rational problem solving and strategy management will not do the trick. We are so overtaken by unanticipated consequences that we think no one is in charge. But someone is in charge all the time, and it is you. Every now and then you must stand back, get out of the way, and let go. Not to the detriment and danger of the people in the school, but to acknowledge that there is some kind of imp in the machine and that right now this is not going to be the way we want it.

Maybe the chaos theory is acknowledged by the gathering of students for practice and rehearsal for major school events. Can you imagine what a graduation ceremony might be if you never held a rehearsal for it? Wow! Would that be outrageous or what? Don't you hold parent orientations so that the mothers and fathers can find reasonable ways to make sense out of all the things that will make the sons and daughters just slightly demented as the kids get used to school? Have you ever tried to keep all the fifth graders away from the windows on the day of the first snowfall?

Here's something to visualize. You and the staff go over the procedures for entering and leaving the cafeteria. It all sounds so clear and straightforward to you and to them. You think that the students will be able to get in and get out, lunch period after lunch period,

without lots of confusion. And to the whole world that may well
be a very nice conclusion. Then the first couple of days of school
arrive, the lunch periods come, and the entire plan is belly up. My
goodness, you might just as well be trying to evacuate a sinking
ship. How did all this craziness develop? It's quite like herding
goats. Well, worry not; the confusion will somehow all go away. Just
give it time and make as few demands as possible upon logic. Oh,
one other thing: Never invite observers into the school when
everyone is at the bottom of the learning curve.

How many of you reading this book have made a master
schedule, conducted a freshman orientation, introduced the sixth
graders to their new middle school? Do you ever anticipate
problems with lots of ninth graders in the wrong part of the
building? Despite what you might tell the new sixth graders,
despite what you might show these wonderful children, do you
ever now and then get slight palpitations thinking that some of
them may get on the wrong bus at the end of the day? Paying
attention to directions that help you locate your bus is very hard
when it is so much more important to look cool.

Once we see that confusion is squarely embedded in what we
do and in the topography of where we do it all, we will get pointed
in the right direction. Once we sharpen our skills to work in the
face of the confusion and mild chaos, then we are on the way to
conquering the things that make schools both interesting and frus-
trating. In any event, here are some things to consider:

- When it comes to rules and policies, be very straightforward and
  very simple in your choice of language. Refer to the ways of
  leaving the building as "How to leave the building," rather than
  "Procedures for School Evacuation." Evacuation sounds
  ominous. With a word like "evacuation," most people think,
  "What's going on here?" rather than, "Which way are we
  supposed to go?" Resist the urge to call it an "Egress Plan."
  The egress business makes people think of birds.
- Figure out what misinterpretations, misunderstandings, and
  confusions are possible. Then build a reaction to those confusions. Play out all those worst-case scenarios. Actually, those

scenarios, if that is what you want to call them, are actually big chunks of confusion that we label with fancy names. The response to chaos comes under the heading of Plan B.

- Remember that less is better. The fewer things you have as part of the buffers against confusion, the less confusing all will be. Have the sign read: "Wrong Door. Turn Around," rather than "This door is to be used only by authorized and appropriate personnel."

- When you set out rules and policies, never give a lot of thought to alternatives. Here's the way it goes. *Question:* Are there any other ways we can do that? *Answer:* No! There is no alternative rule to "Come to school on time." That's it. Once you start with the alternatives and the exceptions, you get confusion. Too often your students and your staff will say things like "I forgot" or "I didn't understand." So here's the rule that will offset confusion: Just follow the rules. What are the exceptions? There are very few. If there are exceptions, you be the one to grant them.

- Stop worrying about inconsistency. Inconsistency is one of the neat tricks of leadership. Who ever said that effective leaders were consistent? One of the great scholars—Ralph Waldo Emerson—said that a foolish consistency is the hobgoblin of little minds. Figure out the meaning of that and then you have the confusion thing licked. The ebb and flow of schools is too irregular and fluid to require consistency. It's almost as though it needs to be confusing to be fun. If you take away the confusion, where's the challenge?

Today's blueprint for action is tomorrow's scrap paper. Do today's plan, then move on. Stop thinking that the agenda for last year's opening meeting will work this year. Look at it, pick what may work best, and get rid of the rest, or start over. Just understand that every now and then everyone, anyone, has the right to be slightly crazy. Logical people who make good plans and inform everyone of those plans in the clearest language also screw up. Working hard at things and being well planned does pay dividends, but not all the time. It never makes for guaranteed outcomes. There is some higher power that watches everything the principal does and every so often that higher power decrees that you have been selected for some form of cosmic throttling. So sit back and enjoy. Make your plans, but make certain that every plan begins with "Stay Flexible." Understand that if the job were so easy and all the confusion had some logical solution, everyone would be applying. Only the strong need seek the job of school leader. Only those whose minds can encompass the confusion and the chaos will ever get the job right. Get your plans; check your to-do list; update your Palm Pilot. Wade in and conquer.

28

Encourage Collegiality

Do you remember the saying about those who play together? Actually, I think the saying had something to do with praying together. Anyway, "If you play together, you stay together." What we need is more "liking" behavior that fosters playing and having fun with the people who compose the faculty, the staff, the "folks." The people who educate children need to demonstrate their own socialization skills. Isn't it amazing how adults seem not to like each other sometimes? I know about all the rigors and all the demands. "Well, you just can't make everyone happy." Why not? What's the problem with trying to make everyone happy?

I also know that no one up there or out there seems to be caring a whole lot about teachers and administrators. By the way, are they supposed to care a whole lot? How much thought have you given recently to the mail carrier or to the guys who pick up the trash? Most of those outside education think we receive too much for too little, and now we want sympathy. Hey, get a life! Why should we deserve any sympathy? We are well paid for what we do! What we lack is mutual support for the things that we do. We often fail to support our colleagues. How interesting it is to listen to the faculty room conversations. And we are supposed to be collegial? Did you hear what some of the staff are saying about our profession? Interesting! Not happy with the job? Don't like what you do? Feel abandoned? Then get out.

Then, of course, too many of the higher education people build repuations by picking apart what public school principals and teachers do or fail to do. You would think that higher education people would take a more benign and loving point of view about public school educators. Of course, if the higher ed people did not have the elementary and secondary teachers to treat condescendingly, what would they talk about? Not a lot of collegiality there. Maybe I should soft-pedal my cynicism, but I have rarely seen a college of education faculty go on record supporting what the public school educators in the town accomplish. If I ever hear about a parade they hold in honor of the good work that public school teachers and administrators do, I will soften my viewpoint.

What we leaders need to do is to help our staff get along and play nice together. We need to provide every opportunity we can for collegiality. Fostering collegiality is the key networking trick. I have the sense that we make a great deal about networking because it suggests latching on to those people who we think have something to offer. I think we gravitate to folks as screwed up as we are and seek reinforcement for the kind of weird stuff that makes us crazy. Or there may be something very, very serious about "networking." Yuck! What a word! Maybe that's the problem. It's too bloody serious in the first place. Besides, "networking" applies to computers, not to people. People do things together that transcend mere networking. People are not easily "connected" or "plugged in." Maybe we need to discover another term that describes our abilities to honor and to respect the gifts of our colleagues. Let's stress mentoring. The word derives from the word for wisdom. "Networking" sounds like a contraption used for snaring fish.

So we build some real collegiality among the staff members. We take part in tribal activities that build upon rituals. We get T-shirts, and school songs, and secret handshakes. We sit around in circles and tell stories of our tribe and its wondrous connections with the fulfilling quests for truth and knowledge. We initiate each other into the bonding rituals that tie us together in an incredible journey. We keep out anyone who does not love what we do. We shun those who cast negative glances our way. We draw from the strength of those who share our purpose and our vision and we use herding up (sound familiar?) to strengthen our purposes.

Here's what we need to do:
- Focus on doing well what we do.
- Stop saying bad things about each other.
- Stop trying to do the other guy's job.
- Seek praise for work well done. What we seek, if our seeking gets results, is feedback!
- Honor the fine efforts of team members.
- Distribute praise in large and boundless measure.
- Diffuse dissension whenever and wherever possible. I'm referring to dissension, not cognitive divergence or more simply holding a different view.
- Close ranks with those who share our purpose.
- Get the job done.
- Celebrate individual and schoolwide success.

Collegiality is defined by the ability of peers to be equally empowered. It suggests equality of purpose and mission. Somehow I fail to understand the strong criticism that teachers in the building have for their peers and colleagues. Does it amount to a way of making oneself better than the guy down the hall? Is it a way to convey that some staff are superior to others? Does it relate to the need for some primitive hierarchy like territorial markings by the strongest member of the herd? Who knows what's at work? I have known the lack of collegiality to go as far as staking claims to certain chairs in the faculty lounge and never allowing anyone else to sit in those chairs. Is that stupid? Is that wrong-headed? Absolutely, and it contributes nothing to collegiality. Collegiality is getting rid of the artificial barriers that keep the English teachers from interacting with the guidance staff. Collegiality recognizes the common purposes and the common goals that all teachers have: to make this school the best place for all of us to be.

29

Seek the Simplest Plan

Here's how good planning works. It starts out in rough form, very general, and sometimes rather vague. The plan assumes some form that allows everyone to take a look at it. At this point, it is still rather undefined, but that's how plans begin. Those affected by the plan fill in the gaps and the blanks with acts of naive behavior. They get some opportunity to have a whack at it. Maybe the participants in the ritual say, "Wow, this makes no sense to me." They may even ascribe forms of brain damage to the originator. But they keep the plan out there in the early stages. They approach their input task in a sort of mind-mapping way. They throw the plan up against the wall to see what sticks.

Planning is an evolving thing that requires some iterations, some strikeovers and erasures. The more the planners work at it, the simpler it should become. Most plans and most planning are so immersed in complexity that it is wondrous indeed to finally discover that anything happened. Planning builds upon a creative urge, an impish impulse that defies logic.

Stephen Covey made the suggestion that we need to begin with the end in mind. Somehow that little gem has interesting implications for those who respect the simple. Here's an end point: "We want the kids to enjoy each novel they read." The planning takes on the form of a quest for the best, a search for the most readable and enjoyable literature we might put in the hands of the children. If we truly start with the end in mind as we work through our planning, we are off to a good start. What will all this look like when we are finished? Good question. You need to ask the staff this question: "After we are finished with the planning, what results would you like to see? How will things here be better?" If no one can come up with a reasonably good answer to that question, you need to get your thinking straight, take a deep breath, and start over.

As we plan, we need to remember that only people who know what they are doing have a right to be in on the planning. For some unknown reason, the democratic impulse has caused school people to include everyone in the planning process. My goodness, we get students involved where they do not belong. We bring board members in simply because we feel that at some point their involvement will save time down the road. Not so. Board members' responsibility is to approve, not to devise the plans. Honor the need to seek advice and ideas and "input"—now there's a funny word—from interesting and interested people. As you plan, avoid entanglement with people who you know will be negative and who always want "to play the devil's advocate." Go try figuring out what that term means in the planning process. Anyway, get the news and the views, weigh carefully the good ideas that sound thinkers produce, formulate a strategy, let everyone in on your strategy, and move along. Keep away from paralysis by analysis. Stay away from all those on the plan-wrecking team.

Two effective skills that you need to put into play as part of the planning process are problem analysis and judgment. Once you determine the "What?" and the "How?" you need to kick in your organizational ability. Problem analysis is securing the best information from the best sources and determining that the information you get relates to what you are going to solve. Problem analysis is problem solving and it relates to effective questions asked of people with good information (data). Good problem analysis works toward a conclusion; it does not go on and on. There is always an end point where one says, "This looks like the answer; that's the way we will go."

Judgment is applying the good information for the best results. Judgment relates to the best consequences for the decision we have made and for the plan we will implement. At its best, judgment reduces the impact of unintended consequences. If there are lots of things that you have not thought of, you need to understand that your problem analysis was faulty. One other thing: There really is no such thing as bad judgment. The correct expression for judgment misapplied or in error is faulty thinking, silliness, and stupidity. Effective judgment eliminates those terms. The poor administrator who made the young ladies at the prom hoist their skirts so she could check for thong underwear was not exercising bad judgment. She was being stupid. Bad judgment is a classic oxymoron. Judgment and all its implications are good; error-ridden behavior is bad.

If you do the problem analysis and exercise the needed judgment, then you have to get all your results organized so that you present them in a timely and sensible way. Good organizational ability goes well beyond what you put in your Day-Timer or enter onto your Palm Pilot. Good organizational ability is what will ultimately make the simple plan effective. Good organizational ability relates to who gets involved, what timelines you establish, how you delegate the things that need doing, and how you will reach the resolution of your problem.

Problem analysis, judgment, and organizational ability move you toward the development of a simple plan. You certainly need to do some other things as you develop your plan and as the plan takes shape. Probably it is good to consider some of the following points:

- Good plans derive from thoughtful behavior. But every now and then, impulse does have an interesting effect.
- The brain and the gut are mysteriously connected. Sometimes one works better than the other, and you just need to figure out which one is functioning best.
- An effective plan does not need lots of parts. Sometimes an effective plan is as simple as "Let's do this."

- You do not always have to scurry around for input. Ask the smart people in the organization what they think of the plan. Then try it out.
- Effective plans need to be easily changed and adjusted. You might ask this question: "What is the simplest change I might make as we move along?"
- The bigger the consequences, the more careful and exact you need to be with your planning.

Maybe the most effective plan is the simplest one presented. It seems that the more detailed the plan, the more the planner and the followers have to remember. The more things that compose the plan, the more things that might go wrong. Simple is better. Simple is easier to check; it's easier to verify; and it's easier to implement.

Keep Every Meeting Agenda to a Few Key Points

Get over the need for lengthy meetings. Stop wasting your time and staff time with meetings that go on and on. Just stop all the gab and all the high-blown rhetoric that really says so little. Keep in mind what you know about long- and short-term memory. The members of your staff are focused on one thing and one thing only—they want to go home. They really do not want to listen to you, as inspired as you think you might sound. Figure out what you need to tell the staff, tell them, and then let them go! Find some clever way to do all the things that need doing without spending inordinate amounts of time with you talking and them listening.

Try beating your previous record for the abbreviated meeting. And understand that those who attend will be vocally critical of your brief meetings. After all, they came prepared to bear witness to the worst. You gave them the best.

Maybe you should have three-item agendas, but I think that some of my colleagues who have an eye for the symbolic would scream a bit. What we are after is a short, focused agenda that gets the job done. There may be no rule about the number of items, but there sure is the sense that long enough is long enough. Most of the things covered in long meetings end up in the lost and unfound pile anyway. We all know that most adults have a hard time with short-term memory. Actually we remember only those few things that touch us deeply and personally. We also know that most faculty meetings occur at day's end when most normal staff members are at tremendous levels of overload and fatigue.

So many principals feel that the faculty is really enthusiastic about sitting on hard cafeteria chairs at day's end. Certainly, most faculty have done nothing so bad that they deserve forty-five minutes of the latest changes to the special education code. They may need to hear something about caring for special needs children. They certainly need not be belabored by chapter, title, and verse of the special education code by someone who is indifferent to how the legislation affects your school. Nor do they need to hear about every meaningless change in the budget proposal.

If you can, avoid giving the union rep, the PTA president, or some central office chap any of your faculty meeting time. Let them call their own meetings, get their own pastries, and brew their own coffee. Of course, you need to encourage your staff to attend the sessions sponsored by your colleagues. And if you do provide meeting time for others, make certain they talk with you specifically about what they intend to present. They, like Elvis, leave the building; you have to stick around to deal with the consequences.

First, we need not waste our time; second, we need not waste staff time. Look, we all have much better things to do. Hold meetings only when there is a need to do so. If you think meetings have some great symbolic significance, hold them only on days that mark seasonal change, or on days when the full moon rises that evening, or on days when there is some other magical thing going on. If you have a need to gather up the members of the group for bonding and building community, do that in some celebratory way. Hold a coffee klatch; play some music; show a short film. Have someone in the group share some exciting venture with his or her colleagues. Never allow the athletic director to talk with the staff about things like the spring schedule or about the way the athletic schedule will affect the shortened day. Refuse the guidance staff time to talk about letters of recommendation or the changes in the state university's screening process. Everyone with a title feels that he or she has something evocative to say. Sorry, it is not so.

Pay attention to some of the following:

- Put only interesting items on the agenda. I am uncertain what the test for "interesting" is. It sure isn't "resurfacing the parking lot."
- Offer a prize for the most creative faculty meeting format suggestion.
- Threaten any faculty member who wants to put something on your agenda. Again, let him or her call a meeting and then see who shows up.
- Never, ever put things called "housekeeping items" on an agenda.
- Do not under any circumstances allow the winner of the student essay contest in the local newspaper to take up faculty meeting time. Hold a special event and have some fun and joy with the winners of anything. But faculty meetings will dampen the spirit.
- Try out your agenda items on some of your really smart key staff members. Get some planning help from a select few. Then honor what they tell you about your meeting plans.
- Last (certainly not least), be extremely circumspect about those dreadful back-to-school opening faculty meetings. Put some kind of bulletin together, brew a pot of coffee, and purchase some good donuts. Focus upon the things that will make the returning staff smile and enjoy being back. But no drawn-out meeting. Have a fair. Do some kind of welcoming activity. Try a cookout. Get jugglers. Make it more than just another meeting.

Have you noticed just how overwhelmed your staff is? Has it occurred to you that your faculty never has enough time to accomplish things? And now you want to have meetings? I like that wording: "have meetings." It sounds like having a headache. I am not denying the necessity of getting staff and faculty together— you have to do that. I am suggesting some circumspect approach to meetings. You need to discover some effective and creative way to get it all done. Meetings add to the madness, they make more work, and they may not be a whole lot of fun.

31

Emphasize Positive Activities

Talking about the positive things takes the cue from Tom Peters, who encourages cheerleading in the organization. The positive talk needs to start with the leader. He or she must always carry a happy face. And I am not suggesting a blind, silly, Pollyannaish manner. I am talking about behaving as though the glass is truly half filled, things are going pretty well, and teaching and being in schools is a pretty noble and ennobling set of activities.

With all the negative talk that goes on in education, it's amazing that we are accomplishing anything. But we are. In fact, we have accomplished some rather amazing things. The sooner those who educate those who need educating start talking about the wonder of it all, the sooner we may change a whole set of expectations and get things moving again. In 2000–2001, public school educators in K–12 schools educated about ninety million students. Now that's pretty incredible.

We have too many experts focused upon the issues that matter very little. We have lots of well-intentioned people who all cast about for the quick fix without understanding quite what they are fixing. The researchers and policy makers seek to remedy problems from a perspective that requires the problems to be valid if not substantial. These gurus need to play school for a while, get with the folks who do the work, and groove on the wonder of it all. What is absolutely amazing to so many of us is that we can teach anyone to do anything, even with the poor support we get. So here come all the researchers voicing protests at my cheap shot. I am sorry, but I wonder why we see no clearer results with all the money, the efforts, and the brainpower directed at the "research problems." Anyone out there notice great strides in reading instruction over the past three decades? Have any of you missed the leaps being made in teacher and principal preparation? Lots of talk with few results. We get a hearty dose of problem identification without commensurate problem resolution.

I am talking about a little horn blowing and a little self-aggrandizement from all those who daily perform public school work. Goodness knows, there are few doing much self-praise. I think we are afraid of repercussions, but there's nothing wrong with a bit of bragging. Look, we have had all the problems paraded before us for a long, long time. No one is front and center talking about the gains. So let's start the cheering and the good talk. Maybe we will acquire some of the momentum that comes from self-fulfilling prophecy. Let's cheer for our accomplishments; then let's reach down to grab hold of the things not working so well and get those things fixed.

My sense is that the researchers and experts could make things better by focusing on the behaviors that make things better. I know we need the TIMSS data. Yes, we really do need that data. I am uncertain that a lot of productive ends have come from all the talk about the TIMSS results. Many experts from some very fine universities have taken lots of face time to explain the significance of the information. Possibly it may not be all that significant to the "grunts" who try teaching the equality rule to kids every day. Who knows? But who really cares that Korean students perform better in math than U.S. students? I have not seen boatloads of moms and dads heading for Korea as a result of that disheartening information. Amen! The mandate to the guys with the great ideas is to identify some miracle in public schools and build upon that success to make some other issue better.

Here are some things that all of us might do to accentuate the positive, talk the good talk, seize the day, and make the community notice what we are all about:

- Make lists of weekly and monthly achievements and put those lists up in prominent places in your building.
- Encourage the staff to share good news with their students and with the parents of their students.
- Do things that bring the parents and the community into your building: hold coffee klatches, have small group lunches, hold sessions that inform the community about your successes.
- With your staff, brainstorm public relations activities that focus upon the most productive activities in your school. Offer incentives for the best public relations ideas.
- Seize every chance you get to brag about your staff. Highlight and promote their activities. Whatever they do that looks like a success, promote that activity.
- Take advantage of the media offerings in your community. Develop a nonconfrontational relationship with the local reporters. Get them into your building and honor what they do so they can honor what you do.
- Get invited to visit with community groups like Rotary, the Lions Club, the Kiwanis, the local chamber of commerce, the church groups—any of them—to make your statements about the wonderful service your school provides. (You may even want to join one of these wonderful community groups.)
- Find interesting ways for your students to do community outreach and community services. Then find a way to make certain that whatever they are doing is talked about openly.
- Develop an engaging and effective newsletter that focuses upon the successes and the gains in your building.
- Seek the help of the men and women in business who know a great deal about public relations. Pick their brains and profit from their insights and knowledge.

Promoting the positive things that happen in your school is not a one-time event; you need to stay engaged in getting the good word out there. It is a hard job that will result in extremely meaningful consequences. The promotion of your good work is much more than a public relations gambit. Rather, it is exercising a responsibility to keep those who pay the bills informed about their school. Despite any cynicism that one might have, promoting the positive accomplishments has really awesome consequences.

32

Support Healthy Behaviors

What is a healthy behavior? Anything that furthers the vision of the organization and the commonweal purposes of the school and those dedicated to its efforts and programs. Now that covers lots of things. It even goes so far as to include any kind of divergence that keeps those in charge on their toes. Healthy behaviors have nothing at all to do with keeping quiet in the face of absurdity or in the presence of stupidity. Healthy members of the organization remind everyone when the craziness begins. Healthy people remind those who lose their center and their focus that they have become slightly (or completely) crazed. Only the brave and the healthy need apply for the job of school leader.

Let's list some of the healthy behaviors that make schools run well.

- Enjoy what you do
- Support each other
- Smile a lot
- Play nice and be fair
- Treat those who come to school with dignity and respect
- Model the best behaviors
- Refuse to accept mean and rude behaviors; your refusal has nothing to do with behavior codes or handbooks

- Talk the good talk
- Listen well to everything
- Show those touched by the school that you care
- Teach with passion and vitality
- Teach as though your life depends upon your performance
- Demonstrate sense and sensitivity
- Love all and serve all

It's quite easy to discern the sick from the well, the quick from the dead. Part of the problem that leaders have contended with for a long time results not so much from the inability to distinguish healthy from unhealthy behavior. Rather, the problem stems from trying to figure out what one does in the presence of really sick, dysfunctional behavior. The question is: How does one deal with the sickos in the organization?

I and many others are puzzled by the presence of the kid haters, slackers, shirkers, trash talkers, noncooperatives, negatives, devil's advocates (they need other deities for whom they might advocate), and the all-around strange people who find their way into schools. Where do all these strange people come from? How do they manage to graduate from colleges of education? Were their supervisors asleep during student teaching? Have their principals been oblivious to their behaviors? Can the teachers' associations and the union reps really advocate on behalf of teachers they would not like to have at their homes for dinner? Guess not. But too many staff, for really poor reasons, circle the wagons around those who need to be guided off school grounds. If we used only our subjective judgment regarding unhealthy employees in schools and dumped most of those without a whole lot of fanfare, we might move the school well up the effectiveness scale.

The weird ones just wander into the schools. Actually, they wander around in the schools, disinclined to center their behaviors on productive things. Rather they prefer to grouse and complain about how the organization fails to take care of them. These are the ones who always decry the total lack of support of administration for the things these whiners do or fail to do. These babies have the feeling that administrators exist solely to buttress their half-baked efforts. These are the ones who limp emotionally into a principal's office to tell sad stories about what some child said or failed to do to comply with a rule that they needed to enforce. Much of what they say begins with statements like "I knew we would get no support for. . . ." Mostly what they seek support for is their own petty agenda that has little to do with the direction the organization is taking. Some of these poor souls seek assistance and support for things that logically they should be able to do. I suspect that good principals with effective interviewing skills can discern these tired and burned-out candidates.

But principals also have to work with the inept they have inherited. Let's not get confused here. I am not decrying the simple presence of the inept. I am cautioning us to be really careful in working with those who do not belong in schools, with those who daily damage the hearts, minds, and souls of those students with whom they have contact. There may well be no developmental program or in-service miracle that will make the inept fit into the demanding role of effective teacher.

Everything, no matter how minor, is an imposition on the sick, tired, and strange people. They like comparing how things are with the way things were. Of course, things were always better then, never now. "When _____ was our principal, these things (whatever that may be) were always taken care of." "Things were always so much better when. . . ." "They certainly do not give us kids like we used to have." And on and on and on. Scores were never lower, kids were never meaner, administrators were never dumber, and life may never be quite as cruel and unjust as it is right now, right here. Everything you ask of the fainthearted and run-down is an imposition, whether that task is defined by the job description or not. And so many of these people are like a gigantic "make-work" project for the association and union support staff.

I suspect there may be rules against some of the corrective measures I might suggest to deal with the lame of mind and weak of heart. But rather than treat these poor rejects meanly, I would propose that we simply get them out of harm's way and encourage them to do something else. A former colleague of mine said there were two types of teachers—the "naturals" and the "artificials." I'm talking about getting rid of the artificials. Let's help them find something else that suits their needs and does not impede the needs of children. These individuals are not professionals even if they can mouth all the professional-sounding expressions. They are unhealthy occupants of jobs requiring the physical and emotional best one has to give.

When we talk about healthy behaviors, we are referring to emotional, spiritual, and mental health. Most schools have sick days for staff who are not feeling well. However, we seldom hear of a school or a school district that provides healing time for staff and administrators who are crazy and nasty. So we need to be circumspect about those in the school who imperil the well-being of others with their mean and abusive behaviors.

Someone—read principal—needs to assist the unhealthy members of the staff to get better or get out. Unfortunately, schools are unprepared to resolve some of the unhealthy issues that confront adults. I know of no school that has a time-out room for big people. They have faculty or staff rooms; those places often tend to be unhealthy. I know that most schools have support for at-risk students. Does anyone offer support and assistance for at-risk employees?

I suspect that with the proper screening, we might safely assume that those we hire are healthy. Then again, that assumption might be tested every so often. Perhaps one of the tests of an effective and an effectively led organization is the ability to deal constructively with unhealthy members of the organization. By the way, keeping the sick staff members in the fold is not the answer. We remediate kids; we do not remediate the adults charged with the responsibility of helping kids. Where do you put the dysfunctional adults who mismanage and abuse? Do you keep them in classrooms so they can continue their path to harm?

We need to be as vigilant as we can be in monitoring the behaviors of the adults in the school. We need to applaud every demonstration of healthy behavior, and we must anticipate and respond to demonstrations of mean-spirited and negative behavior. As the principal, you need to have a plan to counsel those who periodically get into a funk, who simply are not doing well. You need to be the good listener who refuses to say, "I just do not know what to do here." You must have someone available to you who can assist the temporarily dysfunctional staff member to get healthy. You must have the option to use sick leave for broad discretionary reasons. Lacking any recourse, you definitely need the courage and the heart and soul to offer some way out for the damaged staff member.

In most organizations the presence of unhealthy, sick individuals makes others in the organization unhealthy. If you have doubts about that assertion, think deeply about the staff member who spends every free period in the teacher's room and grouses to the detriment of other staff members. What consequences are evidenced by the negative behavior? Who ends up owning the problem? Not just you. Think about the number of students who daily must deal with the off-the-wall behavior. Worse yet, focus upon that staff member who refuses to talk with any colleagues. What's going on here?

What can the principal do to promote healthy behaviors in the school? What steps might one take to bring the entire staff to levels of healthy awareness that ward off the bad consequences of unhealthy behavior? Here are some ideas that you might begin with. Of course, you need to understand that often responses depend upon the circumstances within the organization. Anyway, here goes:

- Do some research so you can determine what constitutes healthy behaviors, those that "talk the talk" or "walk the walk."
- After you do the research, develop a list, a description of healthy behaviors for your school. This is like a "Can Do" and "Cannot Do" list. Once you develop the lists, post them and hand them out. Put them up wherever your teachers gather.
- As the principal, you need to be aware of what is happening with your staff. You need to be on your guard for unhealthy behavior.
- Provide support for the staff by developing mentor relationships so staff can help each other in times of need.

- Come up with a program for the adults called something like "Coaching and Mentoring for Healthy Behavior."
- Offer lots of opportunities for people to voice concerns and talk about healthy practices.
- Stay alert to what keeps the staff well and whole. Provide the resources for the staff and for you to take action about wellness, exercise, relaxation, and diet.
- Do your absolute best to keep the school sane for the adults. Reduce or eliminate whatever elements of craziness you can. For example, provide some nice amenities in the faculty room. Keep the place clean and comfortable.
- Keep the superintendent and district staff apprised of your plans to maintain school and employee health. Seek their support and assistance.

One can probably understand the connection between substantial outcomes and effective performance and the overall health of the organization and its members. I suspect that we make some inappropriate assumptions about the ability of adults to take care of themselves. Most often, adults can maintain and sustain, particularly the high performers in your organization. But every now and then, things happen and people get a bit off center. That's when the principal needs to focus particularly upon those things that will return the staff to balance and health. What the organization does is directly related to how the organization functions. If your school is a healthy place, then the outcomes you seek for your students and for your school will be superb!

33

Encourage Autonomy for Your People

Focus for a moment on the truly functional, happy, intelligent, and dedicated staff. Let's explore an assumption: Intelligent people are capable of leading purposeful and meaningful lives, and they can take on the responsibilities that are part of their chosen occupation. To lesser or greater degrees the evidence (data) that results from simply observing competent people behave, act, and work suggests that supposition is correct. Professional people exercise varying degrees of competence. Every now and then, the supposition breaks down simply because all of us are given to error and to making mistakes.

Observing what happens in schools reinforces the premise that most professionals are competent. To teachers—kindergarten through graduate school—we assign students, assignments, tasks, and responsibilities; we trust them to perform to a set of standards and expectations. Again, simple observations tell us that in the main these expectations are met within reason. Good leaders operate from assumptions that make note of competence rather than incompetence. My goodness, if we start out thinking that the staff will never get this right, then we have asked incredibly difficult things or we have placed too much of a burden on people whose competence is in question. But mostly, principals assume the best and trust the staff's competence.

Another observation tells us that professionals enjoy and thrive in the presence of independence. They like supervisors (principals) to make assumptions that clearly indicate they (the teachers) are qualified, competent, and intelligent enough to take responsibility for what they do. So are we then very surprised that these same professionals bristle at the mindless and silly things policy handbooks, rules and regulations, memos, and directives imply about their evident and assumed lack of professionalism?

Because the entire accountability movement is so poorly defined, we should little wonder why professionals get so terribly upset over the loose and careless discussions about accountability. I have an awful suspicion that those who rant and rave about the need for greater accountability have little sense about how it works in schools. Another lesser suspicion is that the experts assume that accountability is all right for everyone else.

Accountability and autonomy seem to be conflicting concepts. It may be extremely difficult to determine in this chicken and egg puzzle which takes on more importance. I vote for autonomy. It seems that when you develop in your staff feelings of independence within the structure of the organization, you get incredibly self-motivated behavior geared to the essential goals and purposes of the school. It seems that all you need to do is clearly define the purposes, the goals, the mission, and the vision of the school, and then cut the autonomous people loose and let them achieve success.

Here's another really big problem: The control freaks who dominate policy decisions just hate it when the lowly teachers and principals assume the prerogatives of autonomy. Who will keep an eye on those people who think they know what they are doing? Perhaps they need more controls and greater accountability. What the heck was going through the supervisor's head when he or she hired these smart people? Did the hirers think that they really needed to watch over principals and teachers so intently? Then why did they hire them? Did they ever think that it might be good to hire people who need little looking after? I cannot figure that one out.

Do you ever have the feeling that many staff members are unsure of this autonomy thing? Don't you get the feeling that teachers often protest that all you need to do is tell them what you want? Have you ever had a teacher say to you, "Just give me the directions. I'll get it done"? Although teachers talk about their need for independence and autonomy, I suspect both notions in the school setting intimidate many of them. Maybe the reasons are fairly clear. No one has allowed the teachers to "practice" autonomy. Seldom are teachers reinforced for autonomous behavior. Here is where the principal's creativity kicks in and where the effective leader moves ahead in providing sound mentoring for the staff. So let's begin:

- Never assume that the staff clearly understand what autonomy looks like.
- Start by explaining what autonomy looks like. Describe it. Tell teachers how to do "autonomy."
- Be extremely clear with the staff when you provide the broad directions that encourage autonomous action.
- Make certain that staff take charge of their own actions and behaviors.
- Get it clear in your mind that close enough is good enough with some things. Do not get autonomous behavior and perfect results mixed up.
- Know that when you start all that overcorrecting nonsense, you frighten off those whom you want to be autonomous.
- Reward and reinforce all successful autonomous behavior.
- Respond to some questions with "What would you like to do with this?" or with "I am uncertain. How would you deal with this?"
- Create some low-impact events and episodes that allow you and the staff to practice autonomous behavior.
- Stop demanding high degrees of inappropriate follow-up. Quit saying, "Check with me before you go any further." Give the staff space and time to practice their autonomy.
- Do not get bent out of shape when the adults make a few mistakes.

- Create opportunities to talk about the results of autonomous behavior. Maybe the topic of autonomy has to be put on some sort of in-service agenda.

There are lots of opportunities for teachers to be autonomous. In fact, most of their day is marked by independent and autonomous activity. But they may not know they are behaving that way. The classroom is the teacher's domain. Teachers may be slightly intimidated by actions that have an effect on the entire school. Your job is to raise their comfort level so that you are not plagued by constant petitions for decisions that might be easier made at the teacher's level. Encourage autonomy. The results of that encouragement will definitely pay you and the teachers dividends. Keep this in mind: Some of the best decisions are made at the lowest level possible. That's a strategy that speaks to autonomy.

34

Explain What Needs Explaining, Then Stop

Let me share a story. Some time ago, I sat at a board of education meeting in my community. One of the board members raised an issue about the recently released reading test scores. The key word here is "recently." None of us administrators had yet had the chance to examine the scores critically. We had not talked about the highs and the lows (there were both). So this board member asked a question that went like this: "How would one account for the drop in the scores in eighth grade math over the past few months?" An interesting question. Probably all of us were wondering how the scores in some of our grades had fallen off.

The drop in scores somehow needed explaining, but not right then, not at that point. You see, none of us had done any problem analysis. Any answer we gave would have been barking at the moon. So rather than say, "I am afraid that right now I cannot answer that question," my colleague went on to construct one of those remarkable "once-upon-a-time" stories. You all know the kind. These are stories that are pure fabrications designed to baffle and confuse.

The board member was seemingly satisfied. She took notes furiously and a few weeks later bludgeoned my colleague into the ground with his old story that was complete nonsense. As principals, we often think that those to whom we talk actually believe the fabrications that we weave. We make up these stories to satisfy the curious and to keep us from sounding as though we do not know what is going on or have lost our faculties. That is an example of explaining something that needed no explanation right then. Actually, it is explaining something that might defy explanation even in the hands of the most gifted analyzers.

Earlier, I talked about the need for simple policies and simple procedures. The suggestion of simplicity relates to avoiding over-explanation. All of us have this feeling that at times we go on and on talking endlessly about things and events that really require very simple explanations or sometimes no explanation at all. If you do not believe this one, think for a moment about attendance policies. I am particularly fascinated by those policies that convert times tardy to days absent. It goes like this: We keep track of every time a student is tardy for a class and has no good reason for being late. Let's not get into the whole admit slip or tardy slip dance. The student is late. Now if that student is late for school a specific number of times, those late things get turned into an absence. So seven "tardys" equal one absence. On the face of it, the policy seems reasonable.

Return with us now to a very simple arithmetic concept you learned as a young kid early on in school. The concept is the equality rule: as many as you count on one side of the equal sign you count on the other side of the equal sign. Thus seven "tardys" equal one absence. It just does not work. It seems to work even less when you try explaining it to some dad who is really irked because his son or daughter has lost credit or has lost graduation because of an incomprehensible rule. And you have to explain, defend, rationalize, dance around, or lie about that dumb rule. The rule, to start with, is bogus, and you have to explain it. Good luck. You cannot, nor should you. So think about who will be required to explain what as you eagerly impose new rules and regulations. Here's a good question: How easy (or difficult) will this one be to explain?

Here's a question: "Why is my son being suspended for four days?" Here's the answer: "Because he left school grounds without permission." There really is no need to say much more. If you have observed all the little twists and turns that relate to due process, then any other response may well be more information than anyone needs. Sometimes it may be more information than anyone deserves.

One of the staff asks you, "Why is it that I cannot leave school to cash my check?" Now there may be lots of things you might say in response to that question. But long-winded answers that belittle the mental capacity of the teacher may be more insulting than the answer needs to be. It is simply not good practice to allow teachers to head for the bank during school hours. The neighbors will talk. It does not look good. It's a bad idea. But certainly one need not offer a long-winded and detailed explanation. Of course, it goes against the silly side of collegiality—whatever that is—and the softer side of leadership. It just may be true that the best answer is "Your being at the bank at lunch time does not look right." OK. Duck! Here come the bleeding hearts. "If we were truly collegues, then you would allow me to go to the bank."

Principals often tell everyone more than they need to know. So the caution is for the principal to be very wary of questions that begin "Why is it that . . . ?" The list of what might become silly questions goes on and on. The questions are probably good questions; no need to hold a negative view of the question or of the one asking the question. But the questions often trigger a response that seems endless.

Consider the questions below. Certainly, the questions are simple and direct. No problem with that. The problems begin when the responses go on and on and on in an effort to be logical when only simplicity is needed.
- Why were the buses late?
- What is *he* doing in my class?
- Why is it that I cannot spend the art money for a field trip?
- Why did I get bus duty?
- What happened to all the copy paper?
- Why are parents so _____?

Some questions do require specific and maybe even lengthy explanations. But most things are more straightforward and simpler than they might appear. Seek the easiest response, the most satisfying answer, and move on. Simple questions are not presented so you can provide an overwhelming example of your wisdom. So just be quiet.

35

Provide Lots of Feedback

Language experts are critical of the common uses of the word "feedback." Their criticism is probably justified. People like using "feedback" even though it may not apply exactly or correctly to the context of the discussion or satisfy the need for precision. Feedback is used to identify the noise made by speaker systems that are too close to the source of the sound. The dictionary tells us that the second meaning for feedback relates to evaluative and corrective information to the source about an activity, an event, or a process. When we talk about feedback in our educator's world, we probably are using the second of the two definitions in the *American Heritage Dictionary*.

I believe that in the absence of feedback one provides his or her own. When no one tells us otherwise, we most naturally feel that all is well, that we are doing just fine. Of course there are those people who always see the glass as half empty, so they have a rather dim view of things around them. Mostly, we tell ourselves in the absence of signals from "out there" that things are pretty much OK. I suspect all this represents an interesting variation of the "no news is good news" syndrome. Actually, the wording goes something like "No news is no news." It is simply an absence of reaction or response to the present condition of things. Quite simply, no feedback is no data.

In schools, whether small or large, little feedback may be provided to anyone. The students get feedback in one form or another. Of course, it may be a stretch to call the results of regional, state, and national testing feedback. After weeks of preparation and days of testing, students hear very little that makes sense to them about what they just went through. Does anyone think that the kids really care that the teachers might get a pay raise because the test scores went up? Do we really feel that the kids get emotionally warm over having better math scores than some other nearby school district? What does anyone think a kid might say when someone tells him or her, "Your class was in the eighty-sixth percentile"? "Oh, wow!" But that is so far from feedback that it means nothing. In fact, more often than not, it means little to the school or to the district. Face the harsh reality: There are few in the community who will beat your drum with feedback because you did well this year. What they really hope is that you blew it and that they can stand in line to beat up you and your school. Cynical? Not really. Simply informed by the history of such events.

I wonder what schools would become if they were overwhelmed with rich feedback. Part of the problem is that preparation programs for teachers and for principals generally provide little specific instruction in giving feedback to adults. Elsewhere in the book I state that present evaluation models, as developmentally anchored as some claim they are, do very little in offering individuals rich feedback. Oh, you can bet they are filled with criticism, maybe even admonitions for improvement and threats of sanctions. Threats and sanctions do very little in assisting adult growth and development. It is ironic that teaming and mentoring are supposed to be marked by rich feedback and developmental suggestions. In fact there is little to suggest that individuals working in teams provide fellow team members with any objective feedback at all.

To build an organizational environment rich in feedback, the principal needs to do some of the following things:
- Tell everyone in the organization what feedback looks like.
- Describe feedback as content-filled and emotionally rich descriptions of positive and results-oriented behavior. Feedback

really is a form of enriched instructional language characterized by as many specifics as possible.

- Offer staff, students, and parents rich models and examples of feedback.
- Anchor feedback in very specific language. This is not feedback: "You need to demonstrate greater effort working with your classes." That statement lacks content and direction. It says nothing. It is verbal noise. Neither is this feedback to a student: "You need to clean up your act." Rather one might say, "You need to be on time for every class."
- Understand that feedback is usually incremental. In order to effect any kind of change in adult behavior, one has to realize that the thing requiring correction, needing improvement, or sustaining behavior needs to be addressed in little measures and moves. This is a comment to a teacher: "Call on at least three students in every class this week." That suggestion gets more to the point than "You need better student involvement."

A few years back, Tom Peters, the author of *In Search of Excellence*, wrote that feedback was the breakfast of champions. Now, when Peters talked about feedback, he was referring specifically to forms of reaction and response that have an improving effect on the person or organization receiving the feedback. Peters was certainly not referring to the noise and the carping criticism that some think is feedback. The word has lost its meaning in the hands of those mean-spirited people who view any awful thing they have to say as "feedback."

Feedback has an intention: the improvement of actions and behaviors engaged in by the person receiving the feedback. So the purpose is to make things better. An interesting premise of feedback as we use the term is that the one providing the feedback has to possess the skills and abilities to remediate the problem to which the feedback is directed. Think about that for a moment. Someone comes to you as the principal and suggests to you that he or she would like to give you "constructive feedback." Constructive feedback as an expression is a tautology. All feedback by its very nature needs to be constructive, since the motive of feedback is improvement.

Anyway, someone tells you they would like to give you constructive feedback. Get ready for this now—they reach back and fire it to you. In the jargon of baseball, they bring the heat. Before this kind and motivated individual starts telling you what is wrong, you might begin your listening with a key premise in mind. They must have the skill to make right the issues, the action, or the situation to which the feedback is addressed. The feedback provider needs to possess the knowledge and the skill to correct the mistakes you made and set things right. With that premise in mind, you think that the intent of the feedback is both corrective and reasonably benign. But the truth generally is that the person giving the feedback in the organizational setting has some gripe, some complaint, and you are the target of opportunity. And the truth lies in the fact that the one unloading lacks the skills needed to address the deficiencies and make the needed corrections. Generally that is the case.

Feedback is good for people and for organizations. As a principal you need to focus upon the skills to provide feedback and to remediate the staff, the issues, and the activities needing correction.

Fix What's Fixable; Walk Away from the Rest

Schools are places where fixing things is part of the repertoire, an integral part of the activity. No student comes to school with a finished and defined set of skills. Maybe even the principal and the teachers are on the long road toward mastery as they engage in the things they do. Of course, most of us approach the tasks associated with schools with the view that the adults and the organization have the capacity to "get it right." Possibly all of us expect, correctly or not, that the organization called school will function properly. "Properly" may not be the best word. Maybe I mean "right" or "well."

We try very hard to have things in the school run well. In most public schools, things actually do run well. Think about this: Lots of schools are the size of small towns. On any given day, most students and teachers come to school, pursue the day's activities, finish their activities reasonably well, and leave having experienced varying degrees of success. Honestly, most schools are not the places described by the school critics and the school haters. A New York City high school principal told a friend of mine that post-9/11, the population of one high school, was sent to his high school, swelling the enrollment to seven thousand students. Imagine that! The wonderful part of the story was that there were no discipline referrals during the period of increased enrollment because the kids and the teachers knew they had to do things right. Now there's a miracle.

Schools are happy places that impart lots of knowledge, skills, and sensitivities to the young men and women who daily attend them. Schools are organizations where most teachers engage in dedicated and sincere actions designed to make kids smart and ready for the world as they will find it. Each successive generation comments that our schools get worse and worse when, in fact, all the evidence tells us that schools continue to get better.

But things still go wrong in schools and in the school community. Principals dedicate themselves to providing the leadership that will move students and staff and community toward successful goals. And because of the commitment to success, principals work really hard anticipating the things that might go wrong. But every now and then things go wrong and happen in ways that run against the grain of positive actions and behaviors. The negative events grab the attention of the world outside the school. Who wants to watch a news flash about how well the chemistry class completed its laboratory assignments or how the fifth-grade reading class has progressed with its independent reading activities? For the public, that's boring; it's the way it is supposed to be. But when something breaks out, like a fight at the weekly football game or a riot in the middle school cafeteria, then everyone wants to know about those exceptional occurrences. And they are the exceptions, not the rules. Mostly, schools are pretty routine places with little excitement except learning. But now and then the balloon goes up and there are problems. Here is where principals need to get a grip on the realities of being the fixer.

The principal needs to fix or to help fix the things that are fixable. And it is difficult to determine which things can be fixed. The test of what is fixable lies in the judgment exercised by the principal. Here's a problem: the buses are late. Can you fix that? Probably not. Suddenly the power has gone off. Is there something you can do about that? Not really. You can get the technicians and the custodial staff on the case. You can even make certain that the students and the teachers are OK. But that's about all you can do. Some staff member just found some kids smoking in a bathroom.

Can you deal with that? Yes, you can, and you'd better. It seems that there are some pretty clear distinctions between what you can resolve and what you cannot resolve.

Maybe you need to pay attention to the following:

- Get straight in your head the things that you can fix.
- Understand clearly what your responsibilities are and what responsibilities you and the staff share.
- The parents need to get the kids to school on time. The teachers need to get the kids to class on time. The responsibilities are rather clear.
- Every now and then, let the students know what they are responsible for. In fact, make a short list of students' responsibilities and put that list in the student handbook.
- Make that list simple and direct. Here are some things you might consider as student responsibilities. Feel free to add whatever you think is necessary.
  ○ Be on time for school
  ○ Come to school every day
  ○ Respect each other
  ○ Respect the teachers
  ○ Keep the school safe
  ○ Keep each other safe
  ○ Never carry weapons, drugs, or alcohol into this school
- Help the staff with expectations about what they need to do to manage school activities. If they need to be in the corridors during passing periods, then tell them they need to be in the corridors.
- Give the staff the names and the phone numbers of those whose jobs are defined as supporting what teachers do.
- Give the staff lots of latitude regarding what steps they can take to resolve problems. For example, tell the teachers if it is appropriate for them to call central office personnel to resolve problems. If it is inappropriate, tell them that as well.
- Get rid of all the procedures and protocols that pile extra labors on you. Create methods to share the problem resolutions.
- Question everything and anything that gets in the way of simple problem solving. After you question it, get it revised or rewritten.

- Be unafraid to say "I cannot and will not fix that. It is not my responsibility. Nor is that our business."
- Here are some things the principal cannot fix:
  - Negligence on the part of other administrators outside your school
  - Broken and harmful families
  - Abusive behavior by moms and dads
  - Illegal and unlawful occurrences outside school
  - Outrageous stupidity on the part of some adults in your own building
  - Neglected, run down, and broken buildings
  - A lack of reasonable fiscal support for students and for programs
  - Overcrowded classrooms
  - Underpaid teachers
  - Community indifference
  - Political antagonisms
  - Dumb procedures that deny the authority and the autonomy of the principal

So many things happen daily in schools to cause frustration and anxiety simply because there seems to be no solution or resolution. I am not suggesting for one minute that the school leader possessing a strong vision should walk away from issues. What I advocate is fighting the battles that will produce movement toward resolution. Knowing what those battles are is key to expending energy toward resolution. It certainly is not banging one's head against the wall simply because it feels good when one stops. The principal needs to ask, "What efforts on my part will make a difference? What can I resolve?" Once you are clear on that, you know what to do and in which direction you need to move. This is much more than identifying the battles you might fight. It is knowing which battles are your business. Keep in mind the comments about the vision and the mission of the organization. Link your reaction to the responses you should make to this question: Will trying to fix this problem move us closer to achieving our purpose?

37

Avoid the Urge to Overcontrol

Many of our colleagues like this saying: "If you want the job done correctly, do it yourself." Actually, that's not such a bad expression. It works very effectively in a three-person organization. However, it really fails to work in a school of several hundred students, dozens of faculty, several support and noncertificated staff, lots of community members, and hundreds of interactions each day. In fact, the expression for the school leader needs to read: "If you want things done correctly, secure the assistance of terribly bright people." What we are talking about here is the willingness to delegate, to assign a task, and then leave it alone.

Clearly, no one will ever do things as well as you will. You know exactly what "completed" means. You have a perfect picture in your head of what the results of the activity will look like. And you understand just how difficult it might be to get others to see what you see. But go ahead and give it a try. Test your ability to assign and delegate and then to let go of the delegated task. Trust your staff. I have already made this point: You hired these staff members because, among other things, you knew they were smart. If they are smart, then allow them some latitude to do assigned tasks the way they see the assignment or the delegation.

I suspect that overcontrolling (read micromanaging) is the result of an inability to delegate successfully. It is also a lack of trust. It may also be an admission of sorts about your inability to trust your own perceptions of others' ability. Some of us want to be in charge of everything. We can't be. So we must delegate, and for many, delegation is a tough skill to master. Listen, it may well be easier to just go ahead and do the thing rather than try to describe what needs doing. Somehow that feeling lessens the opportunity to teach others what you know. It weakens the mentoring role. And it makes others feel your lack of trust.

Generally the concept of "control freak" is a pejorative one. People in organizations usually keep lots of distance between themselves and the control freaks in the organization. And you know who the control freaks are. Probably you have one looking over your shoulder right now. They all have a particular perspective on most of what occurs around them. Their perspective is colored by the desire to have everything in their world be evaluated according to their very narrow view of what correct, right, and perfect look like. Warren Bennis refers to these people as "small minded clerks travelling in very narrow orbits." They judge everything by the inclination to have it look the way they need it to look.

Most of the behaviors associated with overcontrol are linked to more surface behaviors or issues. Schools are great places for those needing to be in charge simply because there are lots of things that need controlling. But avoid at all costs the urge to overcontrol. That urge will make you nuts.

Go back and reread the observations about the nonrational perspective in your school. How can you get things to align that just defy alignment? Curriculum alignment is a really nice concept, but it is built upon the metaphor of learning and managing learning as a string of beads. Rather, learning and the curriculum are more like a bunch of grapes. Now that might be an unacceptable metaphor in lots of ways. But there may be less logic to learning and less order to the curriculum than we would like to accept. I have often wondered if the people living in Mexico speak

Spanish II. Is there some logic to teaching geometry before Algebra II? It may well satisfy the requirements for orderly movement through the curriculum, but it probably need not get confused with a simple desire for control.

The urge to overcontrol denies a sense of the big picture. Don't you think that you do well whatever it is you do because you have a grasp of the big picture? Your school with its myriad components is an aggregate of so many discrete and separate acts that it quite boggles the mind to describe it all. As the leader, your task in part is to make certain that all the people who come to the building every day understand the part they play. And that is why I have encouraged you to consider describing the responsibilities in both general and specific terms. When general descriptions will work, you certainly can be as general in your descriptions as you like. You need to be specific when you know being more specific will produce better results. And that's about the best you can do. Declare your expectations, describe what you need done, and then get out of the way.

You need to make certain that you are not tempted to over-control. You must reread the manuals and policy books to ensure they are not characterized by highly controlled, narrow, and restrictive language that makes all who read them feel stupid. If the staff and the students and the parents are made to feel stupid, they will really get angry.

38

Plan for Change

There are few places in our society that show an inclination for change better than schools. Despite our yearnings for things past, we educators know that our profession, our students, our teachers, and our daily lives are marked by change. Sometimes the changes are quite gradual; often change occurs almost instantly. A large compartment in our tool bag is devoted to the devices that will create change and help us deal with change.

I suspect that anyone who has taken on a principalship has come to the assignment with some changes in mind. "Things will be different in that school when I get there." "I cannot wait to get my hands on that school so I can try out some of my plans." "I hope that the new school is ready for what I would like to get done." All those statements ring true and all point to strongly motivated desires to move the organization through a period of change that will bring the school to exciting and productive ends.

Change is what we do as educators. Change is what we are all about. The more things change, the more they. . . . No, not remain the same. The more they change. The cliché about things remaining the same is just that, a cliché. Nothing remains the same, and the sooner principals, kids, and teachers recognize that, the easier will be the transitions toward success. Of course, some of the incredible difficulty adults experience in schools stems from the refusal of the "system" to stand still. As the advertisement suggests, "This is not your father's Oldsmobile." No, sir. It's a new day—every day. And the effective principal welcomes and embraces change. He or she strives to get teachers to accept and embrace change. There may well be little alternative these days. Could anyone possibly have anticipated the changes caused by the 9/11 events?

Before we move further into this brief discussion of change, let's take a moment or two and consider these questions:

- What's going on in your school right now that you can do better?
- Is there a particular routine in your school that you could change quickly or get rid of and in the end do no damage to the school? Name it! Describe it!
- What is in your student or faculty handbook that you may not need?
- What things should you stop doing that would truly improve the quality within your school?
- Can you name two or three smart people in your school (or school district) who really know how to manage change?
- Meaningful change may best take place on the "edges" of the organization. Does your organization have edges? Where are the edges? Who's out there?
- What do you do in your school that encourages attempts leading to change?
- Can you name a couple of things you have already done that show you are a seeker of change?

There are some rather straightforward steps one can take regarding change in the school. You may think that you need to be a futurist or some kind of great thinker to engage in all the processes that create effective change. I like the descriptor that I heard used by a consultant friend of mine. She described herself as a change agent. That brought to mind the guy in the arcade who had that little tubelike machine on a belt. The change agent would push down on the little levers and would get nickels, dimes, and quarters to pop out. Now that's a change agent! Most of the good changes may well take place that easily. We just seem to be confounded by the concept because it does look very scary.

Being a change agent is certainly more serious than I describe it. Or so it would seem. Change is a natural phenomenon. So I list for you some of the things that a leader might do in effecting change:

1. **Let your enthusiasm for the new idea show.** Hoist the flag. Beat the drum. Practice your best forms of promotional behavior if you want to sell change. Make it look as though change will be the best thing that has ever happened to your school. Encourage the creative people in your building to think seriously about change activities. And when they do, get excited about what they are proposing. If you cannot adopt a can-do attitude, if you cannot get excited and passionate, then abandon the idea for the time being. Set out some expectations that speak to issues of success and gain. Emphasize the positive and productive features of your proposed changes. Never, never talk about the problems you might anticipate. Too often the "harsh realities" that intrude upon your dreaming have such a bad effect on the dreams, so talk the upside, not the downside.

2. **Pre-sell the change to the key people.** Are there people on your staff who truly are the "key people"? Find them; sell them. Co-opt them and bring them enthusiastically into the fold. The concept of the "trade-off" suggests your need to make a trade to garner support. So what? What's the big deal? If you can get the shakers and the movers on board with some hot change idea, all the better. Once you have the names of the influential people on your list of supporters, then set the stage for their "buy in." Talk in ways that make the big guys think the idea is theirs, that they own a part of your ingenious proposal. Give them a piece of the action. Of course, once you have cut the deal and have them on board, you need to be rather specific about what you want from them. Let them know what the supportive actions look like. What you need early on is blind trust and support. So show what that all looks

like and define your expectations for your key people. You may want to go back to the section on loyalty before you read any further.

File this thought away: Waste no time with the negative staff members. You cannot sell them, you never will sell them, but they will ultimately have to come on board. If the change idea is a good one, it will probably be irresistible. So cut no slack here in trying to convince those of little faith. Spend your time with the supporters, the advocates, the bright and the informed.

3. **Explain all the reasons for the change.** What are the selling points? What things must you say? How might you describe the change in the most irresistible way possible? Practice effective communicating. Be as specific as you can in describing how the process and the anticipated actions will result in great outcomes. Be graphic and brief. Strike a balance between the vision and the more mundane issues. Of course, you need to talk about how the change relates to the school's vision. However, you need to make certain you talk about how the smaller issues will be resolved. But do not allow anyone to drag one of those "insurmountable problems" into the road to success. If the problems look too awesome, don't try solving them. Just go around them for now. You have a clear view of what you want to do, and what you want to do may not relate to someone else's described difficulties or to someone's entrenched history.

4. **Discuss the risks.** Be very honest as you convey the sense that change can get really scary. Most of your believers will never allow you to paint an unrealistic picture. You know how the "Yes, but . . ." responses work. Point out the pain and the pitfalls. You do not need to dwell on the hyperbole, but you do need to know what levels of discomfort your staff will experience and what levels of pain they can endure. If you are going to accomplish great things, you need to make the effort to get the task completed. That's a pretty straightforward approach to change. One last word here: Couch the risks in

personal descriptors. Most questions will relate to how the change and the risk affect both you and your staff. What must you give up? What level of discomfort must you accept? Even your believers and advocates will ask, "What's in all this for me?" Answer the question honestly. Move on.

5. **Announce the anticipated results.** Do you remember Stephen Covey's admonition to begin with the end in mind? Start the change conversation there. Draw pictures of gains and the changes that will produce the best results. Describe the success "look fors," the indicators that will announce that you have made it and it works. If an incremental approach works, then talk incrementally about where you are going and what it will all look like. You need to be able to describe the parts of what you are trying to change. You say things like "First this will happen. Then we will try this, and then this will take place."

6. **Promote what the project is, not what people think it is.** Here is where your sense of clarity needs to be well defined. You absolutely must have in your head the picture of what the change will look like. You more than anyone else will need to answer the questions sounding like "So, what's this all going to look like when we are done?" Of course, you then need to ask those you are bringing along to describe the picture of outcomes they see. Once you get answers to "What do you think this is all about?" you have to bring some kind of symmetry between what you started to work for and what others think you are doing. If some of those on board grow unclear about what is happening, you have to fix the misconceptions. As you move toward the change you want to set in place, there will be lots of perception checks and lots of need to get it squared away. Perception repair is really very important. It minimizes the impact of this statement: "Oh, I didn't think that was what we were doing."

7. **Encourage disagreement.** When you are working for change, you absolutely know there will be disagreements. Actually, disagreement is a process that clears things up. It is a traditional model that starts with "Here is what we will do." Then

someone indicates that he or she would rather do it another way. Then both parties give a bit of ground. It's thesis, antithesis, and synthesis, a really old model, and it works. Most disagreement works out this way. Maybe if the argument does not work out, you are all arguing about the wrong things. There's a real distinction between disagreement and nastiness, and it's easy to tell the difference. Tolerate the former; get rid of the latter. Get the blockers unblocked and get the disagreements settled in very specific ways. Require the disagreements to be set in very specific language; "I don't like it" does not cut it.

8. **Establish some reachable short-range goals.** Set simple goals as you begin the change. Give the believers some tangible point that defines their successful movement in the right direction. It's a matter of simple gains at the outset. Reinforce every initial gain. Get those on board to reflect upon the gain they just made and then allow them to celebrate.

9. **Keep the influential ones on board (or at least afloat).** Is it too obvious to say that the entire change process produces high degrees of frustration? I think that anyone who has ever tried to change anything knows well about frustrations associated with change. Focus, focus focus—the three elements of supporting change. One needs to focus on the influential members of the organization. One needs to focus on the spheres of influence in the organization. And one needs to focus on the level of support provided for the ones who will show you encouragement as you work through the process. Focus keeps everyone on board and contributes broadly to your success with the change.

10. **Stay on top of the process.** Engaging in the change process produces fatigue. People who get excited by change and who are challenged by planning and initiating change get tired. Their attention span gets narrow, boredom or fatigue sets in, and there goes the plan. It becomes really easy to practice forms of passive neglect. One often hears that tired response, "It will be OK." Of course, the whole program will be OK if one pays attention to what is happening. To achieve the end

you had in mind at the start of the process, you need to stay focused and attentive.

So the person leading change needs to pay attention, stay focused, and respond to problems immediately. As one works through change, one needs to know which problems can be addressed and fixed and which ones are just too large, too ill-defined. One of the frustrations of the change process is that you might get really close and discover that things have happened to scuttle the whole project. If the change will not work, if it produces something other than what you wanted, if it is just not going to be a winning situation, then pronounce the horse dead and get off. Then get on to something else.

39

Avoid Fighting Useless Battles

If anyone reading this book feels that fighting battles is a lot of fun, then put the book down and go for a nice long walk. In fact, you may want to walk to an employment agency to get some assistance in either applying for a new job or at least rethinking the one you have right now. Arguing and fighting really consume resources. But is it not amazing how much pleasure some people seem to get from arguing and fighting about things—all kinds of things? I have smiled at the story I often tell about the faculty member who would respond to my comment, "We are having a really nice day," with "Oh, yeah?" Goodness, he was just so aggressive with his response. We all know people who challenge everything and dare us to knock the chip off their shoulder. Ignore the challenge. There are too many urgent and needful arguments to win.

Let me give you a few examples of useless battles. Do not get upset because I happen to put your pet peeve on the list. Having some little things that really bug you is absolutely OK. When the thing that bugs you becomes the hilltop you must die defending, then you need to either get a grip or get a life—whichever comes first. So here are some things that are absolutely foolish to fight over:

- Whether kids can wear hats in school. Sorry, but that really is a weak battle. Who cares about what's on their heads? Let's battle over what's in their heads.
- Whether or not we add two additional minutes to the passing period. Again, who cares? What will cause kids to get from point A to point B safely and sanely?
- Why students may or may not go to their lockers during passing periods. Just set the policy for whatever logical or illogical reasons you see fit and then stick with it.
- Why you should or should not have faculty sign in when they arrive at school. Do it or do not do it. There may be some good reason to have faculty sign in. Just do not demean their professionalism. Signing in may not be so demeaning. In some schools, it's a great way to see the staff in the morning.
- Whether the kids get homework assignments over vacations or not. Stop arguing with the parents, the PTA, or the board—the homework issue is none of their business. As the principal, you and your staff make that call. Don't fight over it. By the way, if the emotional body count goes up in the heat of that dumb battle, then find something else to argue over.
- Whole language? Phonics? I agree both ways. That's an old battle. If you have a strong viewpoint, express it, but don't get in a shoving match over it. Let the curriculum gang fight that one. When they make up their collective mind, tell them to fill you in.
- Battles that affect safety and health issues. You know what it takes to keep your students safe and well. Enforce those issues—never argue over them. If everyone who comes into your building must sign in or secure a pass, so be it. Make no exceptions, not even for the board.

I guess we could go on and on about the countless useless battles that you as principal might be drawn into. While you were reading this section, you probably thought of a few more than I listed. It seems that whenever you are presented with an either-or situation you have a potential argument. You need to be circumspect about what you judge as important or not so very important. Maybe the

test of significance lies in the answer to this question: Will the resolution of this argument move the school and the children further
along in their quest for mastery? If the answer is probably not, walk
away from the argument. Let other great minds grapple with the
unrevealed truths. If the argument concerns the safety and well-
being of those who enter the school, always decide on the side of
safety and well-being.

40

Respect Experience
Wherever You Find It

Here's an obvious statement of fact: On the day you arrive at your first leadership job, practically everyone else in the building has more experience in that building than you do. A harsh reality for you, maybe, but it's true. You are the greenhorn there at the school, and no one there really has to be told that you are the new kid on the block. Additionally, no one there has been breathlessly waiting for you to arrive. The staff may be annoyed, even angry, with the outgoing principal. So here's a guiding principle: Enter with awe!

In case you are unaware of it, a lot of staff are just hanging out there to see how long it takes for you to make your first series of mistakes. They will greet your mistakes with statements like "Well, that didn't take so long!" or "I told you he would fall on his face quickly." Or "What did you expect?" Believe it or not, all of that is all right. Part of the terrain almost requires you to screw up early on in the job. Think about it. You are new here. This is a challenging assignment and it does not come with a set of plans saying "Some assembly required." You must begin by allowing the experience you bring to the job to speak for itself.

You need to remember that you are in that new job because someone expected you to be a quick study and knew that your learning curve would be steep. You are the boss and you are expected to adapt as quickly as possible and to refrain from re-engaging in silly behaviors as you gain experience. One of the great sources of experience is the professionals on the staff. You need to discover who the senior members of the staff are and respect what those staff members know and what help they can provide you. Of course, you probably knew that, didn't you? So all this will serve as a helpful reminder.

We know how so many administrators talk about new staff. One might think that newness was some form of miracle for our schools, but I contend that experience, more than anything else, makes our schools successful. I enjoy the vitality that new staff bring to the job. However, the error-prone behavior that newness on the job brings into the school often drives senior staff and new principals bonkers. So the admonition here is to keep the experienced staff ever present in your thinking as you come to a new school. Here are some things that you may want to do:

- As you begin either your new job or the new year, make some time for the senior staff members. Listen to them. Profit from the meetings.
- Seek out the history represented by the senior staff members. History is a link to the existing culture.
- Remember that the senior staff members were there when lots of the things you are trying to change were enacted. Maybe some of the senior staff were involved in the things you are criticizing. Maybe the senior staff need a way to make the changes gracefully.
- Include the senior staff in your new plans. Never overlook or ignore them.
- Be mindful of the needs of the senior staff members.
- Take advantage of their experience; seek their input.
- Bring them sensitively along through the changes.
- Discover the mentors among the senior staff.
- Profit from the senior members of your school community. Young moms and dads have vitality. What they lack is experience.

- Keep in touch with the senior members of the community to build a context for what occurs in your school.
- Link the beginning teachers with an experienced staff member. Form mentor teams that capitalize on the experienced teachers.
- Provide the senior staff with opportunities to reinvigorate themselves.
- Create some special staff development experiences for the experienced staff.
- Downplay all the rhetoric about how lucky the school is to have hired such bright, shiny new people.
- If you take time to introduce the new staff, make certain you have introduced the senior staff to the new kids on the block.

Some time back, when clinical supervision was all the rage, lots of my colleagues held to the point of view that they needed to expend little time and effort in dealing with older staff members. I never really understood what was at work here. I often thought that I might experience polished and refined instruction by sitting in the classrooms of the senior instructional staff. My belief was borne out. I actually learned more about sound instructional methodology while observing the senior faculty. I guess I had the sense to pass along to the new teachers some of the refinement I observed in the senior staff's classes. Almost by accident I became a mentor for the new hires by concentrating on the skills I discerned and carried away from the experienced teachers' classes.

My advice is meant to suggest that a new principal—new to the job or new to the school—mine the resources that will contribute to his or her success. Linking the experience the new principal brings to the job with the experience discovered in the new building certainly contributes to the potential for success.

41

Keep Track of What's Easily Lost

I put this section in the book and have the sense that its presence almost belabors the obvious. We have so many experts who have pointed us to the ways, means, and strategies of keeping our lives, our offices, our jobs, our families, our events, all of it organized. And poor us, we are so often dazed and confused. First, there is simply too much for us to do. We have learned to love the cult of activity. Unless you are flat out busy, you are subjected to criticism leveled at the slug in us. Then we have all the things in our lives that make us so crazy. Let's not forget all the demands that everyone makes on us. So it surely becomes more hectic and crazy. This little section certainly will never solve all your organizational problems. Its primary purpose is to make certain you give some thought to your organizational skills and make a plan or two to keep the things in your life where you can maintain them without getting crazy.

So let's begin with some questions. You can answer the questions in the margins of the book. You can get your journal and fill it in there. You might also enter your responses into the notes section of your Palm Pilot or your laptop computer. But you really ought to make some notes as a strategy to keep track of your responses.

• What things in your daily life do you typically lose track of?

- Do you use a calendar or a Day-Timer or something like that?
- Do you keep a to-do list?
- Do you cross things off the to-do list?
- Do you keep track of daily events by making notes?
- Do you put things—wallet, handbag, briefcase, keys, spare change, and money—in the same place all the time?
- Where do you keep or store frequently used phone numbers? Do you have a backup system for these phone numbers?
- What kind of organizing devices do you use?
- Right now, look at your desk. What does it look like?
- What does your office space at home look like? Is it organized? Slightly?
- Do you use routine to your advantage? In other words, are there certain mindless things you always do the same way?
- Do you allow others to do things for you?
- Do you pay for services that make things easier for you?
- What are your organizational strengths?
- What are your organizational weaknesses?
- Do you have backups, like spare keys, lists of numbers, an extra few dollars tucked somewhere? Where are those things?

All of these questions either point to the obvious or belabor the obvious, and for that I am sorry. But not too sorry. I want you to focus every now and then on the things in your life that cause you grief and confusion. You will lose your keys. You will forget to pick up your youngest daughter. You will miss a key meeting that your superintendent has called. All of those things and other things will happen. But they will happen less and will result in less dire consequences if you pause every now and then to think about keeping track of the things that easily get lost.

Plan for Stress in Your Life

It has become almost a cliché these days to say that the principal's job is plagued by stress. Whenever someone makes that comment, the responses usually take the form of "Well, tell me something I don't know." Listening to the talk about the difficulty in finding candidates for the principal's job, I suspect that you get to believe more and more that stress is a variable that has a very large impact. A colleague who was recently asked to apply for a principal's position inquired, "Why would anyone want that job?"

No doubt the principal's job is stressful. Maybe his or her job is no more or no less stressful than lots of other jobs. But without any special scrutiny or without a whole lot of research into the obvious, we must conclude that there certainly is a lot about the job that causes stress. The principal, new or experienced, needs to be prepared for the stressors and has to have a well-tuned set of skills to deal with those stressors.

As silly as it may sound, many, many bright men and women pay little attention to the cues and prompts sent from their own bodies. Too many principals, new and very experienced, are so taken with the job that they disregard some of the rather apparent signals that tell them they are hurting and troubled. Here is a set of cues and prompts that might be signals, subtle or apparent, that all is not as cool as one might think.

Physical Signs of Stress
- Dominant body posture patterns
- Clenched fists
- Clenched or set jaws
- Forced posture
- Sudden sweats
- Back pain, neck pain, headaches
- Chronic fatigue
- Stomach pain, gas
- Weight change
- Changes in sleep patterns

Things That Should Get Our Attention
- An obsessive concern for the things at work
- Defining yourself by what you have rather than by what you are
- Refusal to accept the larger environments that surround you. For an unknown or unidentified reason, you seem to be talking more about how little you care for the district or the needs of other schools or principals. This behavior may reflect your inability to be a team player.
- An unwillingness to accept group goals. People who get trapped here say things like "My way or the highway." Stress may manifest itself here when you notice that you sulk and pout. Oh, you thought you were over that. Um . . . think again.
- An inclination to ignore things that fail to reflect your needs. This is the classic "me first" approach to life. For lots of reasons, stressed individuals get this sense that no one else appreciates their needs.
- Refusal to accommodate that which is not defined by self
- A compulsion to challenge rather than to accept
- Defining all challenges in a win-lose pattern
- Explosive, rapid speech patterns
- A chronic sense of time urgency

- An impatience with the speed of things
- Doing everything rapidly—talking, eating, working
- Being constantly on guard; self-protecting; rationalizing
- A refusal to accept newness; resistance to change
- An inability to deal tenderly with yourself or others
- Ignorance of psychological needs of yourself and others

Taking the Edge Off

So what can you do to relax and take the edge off? Are there some strategies that you might employ to give you a shot in the arm and help you get over that hurdle that is there? Certainly there are little steps you might take that will ease the way things are going. Try some of these:

- Get out of your chair and walk around your office. As you walk, remember the ingredients for one of your favorite dishes.
- Learn three or four basic stretching exercises. Stand up and do a couple of those stretching exercises for sixty seconds.
- Take a few seconds and stand in front of your desk. Now straighten up your desk or one corner of it as quickly as you can. Get rid of some of the clutter.
- Sit quietly in a chair away from your desk. Close your eyes. Think of absolutely nothing. Take deep breaths through your nose. Exhale slowly through your mouth.
- Acquire some nice relaxing music to listen to in your office. Take five or ten minutes each day and enjoy that music.
- Sit quietly and name as many of your sixth-grade classmates as you can.
- Name as many of the presidents as you can. Write them down.
- List your five favorite movies.
- Do some "chair isometrics." Press your hands together for fifteen seconds. Do that three times. Suck in your stomach and hold it in for a ten count. Do that three times.
- List five things that make you happy.

There is so much helpful information available to assist any one of us in coping with the stresses in our personal and professional life. Take a minute to visit Amazon.com to see firsthand the useful resources located at that Web site. Each of us needs to seek out the ways and the means to cope. So much of what we do and are expected to do depends upon stress free-coping. No longer can we get by with telling each other how difficult the job is. We cannot simplistically talk about being burned out. By the way, one needs to be on fire to get burned out, and so many principals today have yet to ignite. The issue is embedded in being trapped in a complex situation where one might be asked to perform at unachievable levels. The difficulty of some of these situations screams for us to escape. Maybe many of our colleagues are over their heads. Maybe some of them are unprepared. Maybe a few would be better off in the classroom. Some probably never should have taken on the responsibility of the principalship in the first place. Yes, being the principal is a demanding and exasperatingly difficult job. So only the healthy need apply, and after some time, even the healthiest need support and assistance. We are obligated to take care of ourselves to manage the demands of the job.

43

Understand Ambiguity

Research on stress and the impact of stress tells us that one of the major stressors in our lives is ambiguity. When people are overwhelmed by the feeling that they do not know what's going on around them, they get crazy. Well, crazy may be overstating things, but "being in the dark" does add to the daily stresses of one's life. I think that too little consideration has been given to the vague and ambiguous direction provided to administrators, staff, and community. It no longer serves for the boss to say, "Just give it your best effort." What exactly does that mean? What are we saying when we tell our faculty, "I really do not understand why the budget was defeated?" What kind of faith do we instill in moms and dads when we tell them that we are uncertain about the effectiveness of our math program? All those responses are vague and ambiguous.

So we need to be specific and concrete as often as we can. We need to be the leaders who provide the followers with specific directions and answers. We cannot contribute to the craziness of the situation by avoiding issues with indirect answers. How does "Do what you think best" assist someone in crisis? Maybe that staff member is in crisis specifically because she did what she thought best. Help!

Here are a few thoughts about avoiding the slough of ambiguity and vagueness:

- Take every opportunity you find to respond specifically to questions. When you are specific, you search for facts and data to support your responses.
- Refuse to beat around the bush.
- Never answer a question with another question.
- Do not under any circumstances make things up. Fantasy always results in forms of ambiguity.
- It is perfectly acceptable to say "I do not know."
- Read carefully what you prepare for distribution; be sure what you say is exactly what you mean.
- Make certain that the material your superiors want you to distribute is true and specific. Otherwise, never circulate it.
- Do the policies and the regulations lend themselves to vague interpretation? If they do, rewrite those that are vague and ambiguous.
- Reread your policy manuals and your handbooks to determine each year that these publications never create confusion.
- Tell your staff how you feel and what you feel. Of course, you always need to be mindful of the sensitivities associated with truth and fact.
- Never reward vagueness from a staff member. When you ask a question like "Why have you not called in while you were sick?" refuse to accept an answer like "Well, It was just one of those things."

Schools are places where we thrive on specific responses. We require students to give us facts and data to support their answers. Even when we ask them to talk about a historic event or a wonderful piece of literature, we work hard to get the students to support their views with specific data. Reducing ambiguity is one of the purposes of teaching and learning. Your staff will thrive in a context that avoids ambiguity and builds upon fact.

44

Keep the Organization Healthy

Don't you just know when you are in the presence of sound leadership in a good organization? I think that all of us who have spent any time in schools know as soon as we walk into a building that all is well there, that things work, that things happen for the benefit of those who walk in the front door. The building conveys a sense of wellness and purpose.

On the other hand, you always seem to know when you have entered the "Twilight Zone" of buildings. Red Skelton used to have a wonderful line where he talked through his nose and said, "It just don't look right to me, man! It just don't look right." You need no clipboards with checklists. You never need to have long introductory explanations to what you are seeing or sensing. You just know that something is wrong. Your intuition tells you that just about everything in the environment is out of sync. Most principals have reasonably effective sensory radar. You just know that the place is a bit off center, that things are cockeyed.

There may be some very obvious and demonstrative indicators that this building and this organization are healthy. The signals are neither subtle nor obtuse. Health, wholeness, and sanity characterize every school that is well managed, irrespective of leadership style, or neighborhood, or staffing. Forget all that nonsense that suggests you just cannot achieve organizational health with this staff or in this neighborhood or with these kids. Are not all kids entitled to work, play, and learn in a healthy environment? Shouldn't every staff member contribute daily to the healthy effectiveness of the building and its occupants? Absolutely! to both questions. So what makes it all work? Here's another one of those lists. Check it out!

Healthy organizations (read schools) are described by the following:

- The building and the adults in it are clean and orderly. As you walk into the building, what do you see? And never mind about the age of the building. Is it clean? Are the floors bright and shiny? Does it smell? Is there glass in the windows? Are there chains and locks hanging off things? Is someone moving out or moving in?

- Healthy buildings and healthy schools are permeated by a sense of purpose, and a strong sense of purpose is never defined by junk on the outside and the inside of the building. There are no loiterers. People are where they need to be. Forget all the open campus nonsense. What are we running here, a school or a train station? Listen, you can have flexible schedules and flexible hours. You can have block scheduling. You can run a year-round schedule. But when the whole thing looks like a column of mobs coming and going, then something is quite wrong.

- In a healthy organization, people project a sense that they know what they are doing. Here's a possible response: "When you hire professionals, they know what they are doing." Really? Curious, then, when you arrive at some schools, even your own, that many of the adults have that "deer in the headlights" look. Healthy teachers in healthy schools always look confident, engaged in the school's activities, upbeat, and together. You as the leader own the responsibility to make the staff assured in all that they do. That's your job! And the competent activity of the staff is what defines your leadership. If they look and act like dopes, then look to the principal and tell me that he or she is not a dope. I doubt it!

- In healthy organizations, the professionals look like professionals. What is all this stuff with dress-down Fridays? Help me understand that one. It's kind of comical when you arrive in a school, particularly a high school, and cannot distinguish the students from the faculty. What I am talking about here is a pride of appearance because the adults represent the vision and mission of the school and function as great role models. Brittany and friends might look really cute with their body parts falling out of their clothes. But teachers dressed in nonprofessional ways look pretty silly. Think about this! Maybe the public at large has lost some of its respect and regard for the profession simply because some of the moms and dads watch the leadership and the staff arrive at school every day looking a bit foolish and maybe even slightly bizarre. I'm not tooting the horn for dress codes and all that. What I am beating the drum for is simple professionalism leading to health in the organization. How do you have casual Friday when every other day of the week the teachers look as though they have stepped way over the boundary of casual?

- Healthy organizations are populated by happy people. No doubt, teaching is a hard and demanding job. But is teaching a reason to look like you have lost a best friend? So many principals and teachers walk into the building looking like they are headed for execution. Pick up the step. Put a smile on your face. Greet the world with your best stuff. Be happy. Actually, teachers and principals work in pretty safe places, heated or cooled, protected from the elements, and rewarded with money. Not too bad. When you have to turn out the staff to go hunting for their lunchtime meal, then let's allow them to be a bit cranky. Until then, keep the organization happy by being a happy, well-adjusted member of the organization. Oh, and require all the other adults in the building to behave in happy and positive ways.

- Healthy organizations are characterized by kindness. Anyone who visits the building, comes to call, or needs assistance will be well served. Does anyone who needs to call your school say, "Oh, my goodness, I would never call that office"? And if and when they call or visit, does someone in the organization act as though he or she is happy to see the visitor?

The moms, dads, and other adults are not the bad guys. The bad guys are probably hunkered down somewhere and you will never locate them. They don't like you, your teachers, or the school and will do you dirt in insidious ways. The bad guys are certainly out there trying their best to undermine what you do. They are the ones who call for degradation of free public education by hoisting the flag of alternative schooling, home schooling, charter schooling, and all sorts of well-intentioned methods to take down public schools. But they may not be represented by those who send their children to your school. So treat those served by your school with healthy doses of love and respect, even when they make you mad. Just be the best you can. You will definitely win them over with your healthy attitude. The well-served members of the community will love you for your kindness and will support you when you really need their support.

- We can safely assume that in healthy and sane organizations, the people who work there are healthy and sane. I hope that is an operant assumption. But these days, who knows? One hears story after story about weird and wacky behavior by schoolteachers and principals. Hopefully this is all fringe behavior, exceptional conduct that never represents the mainstream population of professionals. But, then again, there are some truly nutty people who work in schools. Our obligation is to get them out, to get rid of them. Quit talking about developmental activity to bring them back into the orbit of safe and kind behavior. You could probably more easily bring the *Soyuz* space vehicle to a safe landing than bring some of the nuts back to stability. Oh, I know how cruel that sounds. Get real. Malfunctioning people do not, under any circumstances, belong in schools influencing kids. That's so subjective, and who is going to make that call? But if it looks nuts and acts nuts, then it is nuts. And it is the principal's job to be the gatekeeper separating the healthy from the unhealthy. No organization can thrive and grow with maladapted people working there.

- Functional organizations, healthy and happy organizations, are populated by people who trust and support each other. The members of healthy organizations are bound together by mutual and supportive purposes. Everyone in the school wants every child to learn and to be his or her best. All the staff want their colleagues to be their best, the most effective teachers they can be. The entire staff wants the kids to be the best sons and daughters, the best athletes, the best essay writers, the best readers and spellers. In healthy organizations no energy is wasted in moving toward any goal except total success and effectiveness. No one is written off; everyone is brought in.

Is that an ideal, a picture that represents a better condition than what we have? Yes. Is it a bit unrealistic? A bit. But then again, that's part of what makes education great. Teaching and learning and public education constantly strive for the almost impossible. Healthy organizations sell and promote idealism; that's what education is all about. Sound public education has to provide strong doses of the most outrageous idealism we can promote. The pragmatic part of your brain needs to focus upon the number of available textbooks, the salaries paid the teachers, the safety of the building. The idealist quadrant of your brain needs to focus on the dreams to which educators are dedicated. How sweet the prize whenever we get there. In case you have not noticed, we get there a lot.

So in summary, here are some questions designed to guide you toward an assessment of health in your organization:

- Are the school and its facilities clean, orderly, and safe?
- Do the people who come and go have a purpose? Are their behaviors purposeful? Or do they just hang around?
- Do the people in the organization know what they are doing? Are they competent?
- Do the professionals look like professionals and act like professionals?
- Are the people in the organization happy people? Do they bring their best to the job?
- Does everyone in the organization show kindness for everyone else in the organization?
- Are the people in the organization sane?
- Is there a sense of mutual support and trust? Do these people help each other?

- Is every staff member dedicated to the well-being of those who come to your school?

Somewhere in your leadership training, you probably encountered discussions of task and consideration as components of leadership. At one time there was lots of talk about these two components that mark the behaviors of leaders. I suspect that the health and hygiene of a school depends a lot upon the consideration the leaders demonstrate for everything that makes up a school. Consideration is a good thing. In many ways, demonstrating high consideration for the hygiene of the school might take care of some of those elements subsumed under "high-stakes tasks." My premise here is that when you focus upon health and well-being, so many things take care of themselves. I would guess that you never get high performance in unsafe and unhealthy places. Safe, clean, and healthy may take you over the top.

45

Understand What Is There When You Get There

Those seeking the principalship know what is involved in the job. By the time one reaches the point of seeking the position of leadership, he or she has spent lots of hours in schools dealing with the peculiarities of the schoolhouse. To suggest that the aspiring or experienced principal is vague about the position or the elements of the job is naive at best. However, it serves well to remind anyone who takes the job that some things often sneak up on the principal and actually surprise the school leader. Every now and then our colleagues say, "I really never thought it would be quite like that!" And the "that" of the exclamation might be one or any number of incidents.

We know from conversations with incumbents that the job seems to get more and more difficult. Well, maybe "difficult" is imprecise. We do know that the principal's job has certainly grown more complex and more demanding. Maybe we need to bring the position back to levels of control and "doability" that marked the job some time ago.

Maybe the complexity of the job mirrors the complexity of the lives led by all touched by the school. Certainly so many social commentators have given us some rather wonderful insights into the growing complexity of contemporary living. It could be that the changes in the schools are reasonable given the way society has moved along during the past couple of decades. Here are some things that we know for certain:

- Our public schools educate more students these days than ever before.
- Free, open, and public education feels more responsible for social issues than ever.
- Educational issues have grown more complex, particularly in the context of more demanding accountability.
- Taxpayers are more vocal in their reluctance to assume the burdens of public education.
- Public education annually accounts for greater percentages of expenditures of tax dollars.
- Each year, programs for students with special learning and social needs consume more time, more energy, and more money. The advocates tell us that we need to do more. The critics tell us we do too much.
- Noninstructional programs take up a larger share of time in the daily schedules of children and adults in school.
- Teachers are required by legislative enactments to demonstrate their skills and abilities.
- Principals are asked to do more with less. That's a bit of a cliché. However, I suspect that anyone reading this can provide his or her data to support that generalization.
- School construction costs have risen in the parts of the country experiencing rapid growth. Those costs may well take funds from other worthy educational efforts.
- Where they exist, older buildings are falling down, outpacing the ability of communities to meet the demands of required repairs.
- Fewer and fewer qualified and certified educators are seeking principals' positions.
- The critical voices rail against the methods of preparing teachers for entry into teaching. The critics insist that teachers and administrators are underprepared and unqualified for their assignments.
- The national focus for public education is distracted by what looks like enticing alternatives such as vouchers, charter schools,

and home schooling, all of which demand attention from the taxpaying citizens of our nation.

- Our national legislative leaders lack the will to focus intensely upon education and its growing needs. They talk about their educational agendas, but the more removed they get from their campaign promises, the less engaged they are with educational issues.

- Communities eat up their leaders. Look at the statistics on superintendents' and principals' brief tenures in many places. Consider how difficult it has become to find principals for job openings.

It is clear that I could have included many other general issues. In fact, I may well be criticized for leaving out one or two of the reader's favorite topics. Sorry for that. The point here is that all these issues that have an impact upon our schools are constant and changing. Together and alone they create interesting pressures on those who show up to lead and to teach in our schools. Most of our principals and teachers know and understand various pieces of the generalizations I have provided. And they know these things even before they arrive on the campus. There may be no getting away from the conflicts created by competing issues. To make matters even more difficult, the competing forces change, and what was important yesterday may well be passé tomorrow.

How does all this relate to the principal? The principal must work within the context of all these issues and agendas. Then there are the day-to-day issues facing the school leader as he or she provides leadership. Let me share some of those. The good reader may be critical of my listing the obvious. But the obvious may well be discounted simply because one might say, "Goodness, I know that!" Whether you know something and have the skill to act on that knowledge may be very different. The known, the examined, the considered always beat the unknown, the unconsidered, and the unexamined. Any principal, regardless of his or her experiences, who fails to pay attention to the context of the school and to what impinges upon the school is certainly in for a rough time.

So at the risk of beating the obvious into the ground, you have to pay some attention, no matter how slight, to some of these realities imbedded in the school organization:

All the adults who work in your building will at various times be distracted and lost because of their own very personal and necessary needs and desires.

- At times, you will not have all the answers. And your efforts to have all the answers will frustrate the life out of you.
- Remember Murphy's Law and all its corollaries: If something can go wrong, it will. And it will go wrong at the wrong time. The good news: Good planning will usually buffer the problem.
- Schools are and always have been difficult places to administer. It's a bit like herding cats, but the job is still fun and is still rich with rewards.
- No school board will ever pay you or the teachers what you think you are worth. Get over it and go do the job.
- There is no screening and interview process that will spotlight the whiners. Most everyone looks normal during all the stages of interviewing. Not all of them will be competent. By the way, letters of recommendation are often misleading.
- Many native English speakers fail to understand simple expressions in their native tongue . . . or so it seems.
- Things that happen day to day in schools really anger parents. Why? Who knows? But moms and dads sometimes get mad at what teachers do.
- People just do not show up every now and then, and sometimes when they do, they fail to bring all their tools. It's kind of like the room lights are on, but no one is there.
- Schools run out of resources; the copy machine runs out of paper; staff (and you) run out of patience.
- Holidays and full moons have an incredible impact on crowded environments.
- Data sometimes make no sense. Very often intuition works better. When intuition runs counter to the data, go with your gut feelings.

- The job you learn to live with is not necessarily the one you signed on for. If the job fails to work for you, quit. Move on.
- You will probably have a greater impact on the school than you can imagine right now. Persist because persistence pays off better than most things.

So, what do you think? Do you want the job? Did you bring your own brand of the right stuff to the position? Can you believe that being a principal may be more difficult than being an astronaut? The astronauts had Houston to bail them out. Where do you go when things start to fall apart? Are your superintendent and your board equipped to bring you home safely? Who knows?

But there are some things we do know about the job. Here are some of them:

- The community needs you to take care of their children.
- Public education is the greatest bargain in the United States.
- Despite outrageous stories to the contrary, principals and teachers understand kids better than anyone.
- Schools are the safest places for children.
- Public education is still capable of working miracles.
- Public schools do things better than private schools or parochial schools. They have to do it for more children and do it with fewer resources.
- The principalship is a more respected position than you might think.
- The principalship will become even more respected when we get our collective acts together and assert our own significance.
- Being a principal is the most fun you will ever have!

A Checklist for Principals

Checklists work well in the hands of competent leaders. Principals could certainly use a checklist to keep focused on effective behaviors and good practices. A principal might also examine the checklist as a handy guide about skills needed, directions, activities, the day's focus . . . whatever. Pilots, no matter how often they fly, use a checklist in preparing for take off and for landing. The pilot uses the checklist to determine that he or she has followed best practice.

Here's a list of specific skills, suggestions, and practices that might serve the practitioner well. Of course, some of these look familiar; you read many of them in this book. I put them here to remind you about some of the things that get lost, that escape, that get overlooked. Listen, your job is difficult, so the checklist may serve well as a reminder. These items consist of things that you need to do to keep yourself headed in the right direction. These items might also get you to respond, "I have not thought of that in a while." So here you are. Here's a list of things that, if kept in mind and followed every now and then, might make your life a bit easier and might improve your chances of being a bit more successful in handling even the simplest tasks:

- Bring your best to the job every day.
- Show your staff members how much you enjoy what you do.

- Demonstrate how much you care about all the things that happen in your school.
- Talk about your staff as "my staff"; the expression demonstrates pride, not ownership.
- Take both responsibility and credit. If you must, accept responsibility for the negative things that happen.
- Learn to passionately promote the good things and take credit for the positive.
- Every day, talk about the importance of educating your students.
- Never be critical of the superintendent in front of anyone even remotely touched by the school system.
- Seek behaviors to compliment as often as possible.
- Be clear with your directions. Leave nothing to chance.
- Be specific with your praise.
- Understand the importance of positive feedback.
- Never lose an opportunity to provide feedback.
- Teach your staff the importance of feedback.
- Encourage the staff to be positive with students.
- Demand that staff help run the school.
- Make certain that the custodial staff keeps the building clean.
- Encourage the staff to see cleanliness of the building as a part of their responsibility.
- Refuse to allow others to blame "them." (Make certain the staff knows who "they" and "them" are.)
- Make certain the support staff understand their assignments in your building.
- See that broken things in the building get fixed quickly.
- Include the custodial and office staff in the decision-making process.
- Never use "the budget" as a reason for failing to care for what happens in your building.
- Demand professionalism from the front office staff.
- Do not allow the front office staff to be rude to students.
- Make certain anyone who answers a phone in your building knows how to convey a cordial message.
- Get the grumblers to leave their "personal baggage" at the front door when they arrive for the day.

- Let every adult in the building know that students are "the customers" and require undivided attention and care.
- Protect your staff from crazy people in your school district.
- Remind those who will listen that sound educational practice demands better than someone else's uninformed opinion.
- Work hard for those who pay your salary.
- Make certain that all staff on the payroll work for the money they get.
- Be respectful of board members.
- Avoid being forced into an opinion, particularly when you do not have one.
- Every now and then have no opinion. It really is OK to say, "I have no comment about that."
- Having no comment does not mean you have no opinion.
- Never be afraid to say, "I don't know." You can also say, "I don't care."
- When you take a risk, make certain the odds of success are on your side.
- When you use expressions like "pressing the edge of the envelope," make certain you understand the verb "pressing." Also know where the edges are.
- Never tell or join in racist or sexist jokes.
- Avoid assigning blame; fix the problems as quickly as you can.
- Greet your staff each morning.
- Avoid interruptions when you are with someone else; that person may begin to think that the interruption is more important than he or she is.
- Try to see your staff members individually before they leave for a vacation.
- Fight "edubabble" everywhere in your organization.
- Always use the correct, proper, and simple word.
- Dress so that others think you make a good professional appearance.
- Avoid dress code battles; set a good example with your appearance and compliment others who look nice.
- Never miss an opportunity to honor and praise good behavior.
- Understand that good behavior does not necessarily derive from lots of rules.

- Acting nice and treating others respectfully has little to do with policies.
- Never accept dangerous and antisocial behavior from anyone who enters your building.
- Keep school policies simple; interpret board policies broadly.
- Teaching and learning are not politics; never have been, never will be.
- Have zero tolerance for adults on your staff who abuse their colleagues.
- Work to get rid of the adults in your school who behave abusively toward students and colleagues.
- Treat those who "have no time for students' personal problems" as though they fail to understand their jobs.
- Do not waste your time with incompetence; adult development is only for those who can develop.
- Remind the incompetent staff that your job is to get rid of them.
- Do not allow others to write rules and policies that you must enforce.
- Despite what the popular view might be among some staff, there is such a thing as a bad teacher. And bad teachers are bad for children.
- Interview or at least visit with anyone who may be assigned to your building.
- Never be afraid to ask for help.
- Hire smart people.
- Avoid being overly impressed with letters of recommendation.
- Spend some time each day in classrooms and pay attention to what teachers do.
- Meet with students in groups. Talk with them; do not preach.
- Every now and then you will run up against a bad kid. Show understanding, compassion, and strength.
- Speak gently.
- Speak correctly.
- Be brief.
- Take nonemergency phone calls after the kids go home.
- Convince the superintendent that you are not always at his or her disposal.

- Give some serious thought to Tom Peters' notion of "managing by wandering around."
- Try not to run out of supplies.
- Try not to run out of patience.
- Never allow a central office clerk or bureaucrat to make decisions that affect those in your building.
- When the policy conflicts with your common sense, trust your common sense.
- Attend the meetings that the superintendent calls.
- Read good literature as often as you can.
- Talk about education with your teachers.
- When someone starts to complain, ask that individual, "What specifically would you like me to do?"
- As the students leave school, stop one or two and ask each one about a homework assignment. If you get no response, then go talk to the teacher.
- Make certain that teaching consumes most of the assigned instructional time.
- Avoid saying, "If they don't like it, it's their problem." Whatever "they" do not like might become your problem.
- Resolve the small issues immediately; take a bit more time with more complex issues.
- Keep your feet out of your mouth.
- Say nothing rather than say something inelegant.
- Never practice Ready! Fire! Aim!

Appendix B

Leadership Behavior Inventory

An inventory allows an individual the opportunity to focus upon particular behaviors without risk. The inventory helps a leader examine behavior at a particular point in time and reflect upon that behavior as a form of personal assessment. Most inventories are very "temporal"—they capture the way things are at the time one takes the inventory. However, the inventory does provide a focus that may point to needed improvement or to reinforcement. Although we know that no one always acts a particular way, we do know that most behaviors are reasonably consistent. We follow learned or mastered behaviors, more so when we are under pressure.

Listed below are statements that may capture your behaviors in very generalized ways. Select the response that best represents your feelings right now.

	NEVER		SOMETIMES		ALWAYS
	1	2	3	4	5
1. I am comfortable being with teachers in their classrooms.	___	___	___	___	___
2. I am available to teachers needing my help and support.	___	___	___	___	___
3. I can help the staff to focus on the vision and goals of the school.	___	___	___	___	___
4. I know how to reward the people in my school.	___	___	___	___	___
5. I can bring out the best in the people in my organization.	___	___	___	___	___
6. I can serve as the cheerleader for the superstars on the staff.	___	___	___	___	___
7. I know how to resolve conflict in the school.	___	___	___	___	___
8. I can be persistent.	___	___	___	___	___
9. I can keep things simple.	___	___	___	___	___
10. I tolerate disagreement.	___	___	___	___	___
11. I know everyone who works in my organization.	___	___	___	___	___
12. I possess strong convictions.	___	___	___	___	___
13. I can do the difficult work in my school.	___	___	___	___	___
14. I trust my faculty and staff.	___	___	___	___	___
15. I can delegate tasks—even the big ones—in their entirety.	___	___	___	___	___

	NEVER		SOMETIMES		ALWAYS
	1	2	3	4	5

16. I'm easy to find when things
    get difficult.   —   —   —   —   —

17. I openly praise the
    competent in my school.   —   —   —   —   —

18. I provide open and honest
    feedback to the faculty.   —   —   —   —   —

19. When trouble occurs somewhere
    in the school, I go where the
    trouble is.   —   —   —   —   —

20. I prefer face-to-face
    communications.   —   —   —   —   —

21. My subordinates see me
    as consistent and credible.   —   —   —   —   —

22. I am capable of "owning"
    my own mistakes.   —   —   —   —   —

23. I can assist staff members who
    attempt to address and fix
    their mistakes.   —   —   —   —   —

24. I can accept and work with
    ambiguity in the school.   —   —   —   —   —

25. I encourage informal
    groups within the organization.   —   —   —   —   —

I suspect that you might determine that the higher your score is, the better your profile might look. Examine those areas where the score for a particular item is in the 3 and lower range. The lower scores may suggest a problem. Of course, it may be a slight or a temporal problem. However, the lower-scored items may suggest areas where you may want to put some developmental effort.

An Enriched Bibliography
for School Leaders

This list of resources is a compilation of books I have read over the past several years. I make no statements or claims for the relevance of any of the titles listed here. The criterion for inclusion rests strictly on what each of these books meant for me. In some instances, I have included a title simply because I really liked it. Such is the case for Melville and Sophocles. I believe, by the way, that school principals need to read more of the classic literature. However, I have not loaded this list with my biased favorites. If I had done that, I would have included titles by Hemingway, put in more Shakespeare, added a bit of John Dos Passos, and maybe some Sinclair Lewis. Oh, yes, maybe I should have put in a piece or two by J. D. Salinger.

Anyway, some of the titles reflect my personal drives and interests. I love the Carse book. I am very taken with *Henry V* as a study of leadership. *Antigone* really gets to me as a study of the rule of law, as does "Billy Budd: Sailor." Both these works suggest some interesting reflection about rules and policies. I share this bibliography with the hope that, like the note in the bottle, it may float out there and be retrieved by someone who likes books and who enjoys reading. My contention is that busy school administrators have little time for enriched reading and therefore do very little of it. So much the pity for them, for their students, and for their schools.

This list of resources is a work in progress. I have added some titles as I have worked on this book. If you like the bibliography, pass it along to someone else. Better yet, send me an e-mail at Ray518@aol.com. I'll send you the bibliography as an attachment so you can add some titles and maybe edit the list to reflect your preferences and your interests. Whatever you do with this, however you interact with the list, I hope that you get some joy and some pleasure from your reading. I also hope that your reading provides you some new insights and perspectives on leadership.

• • •

Adler, Mortimer J. *How to Read a Book: The Art of Getting a Liberal Education*. New York: Simon & Schuster, 1967.

Bennis, Warren. *Why Leaders Can't Lead*. San Francisco: Jossey-Bass, 1989.

Berliner, David and Bruce J. Biddle. *The Manufactured Crisis: Myths, Fraud, and the Attack on America's Public Schools*. Reading, Mass.: Addison-Wesley, 1995.

Bernstein, Albert J., and Sydney Craft Rozen. *Dinosaur Brains: Dealing with All Those Impossible People at Work*. New York: Wiley, 1989.

Blanchard, Kenneth, and Norman Vincent Peale. *The Power of Ethical Management*. New York: Fawcett Books, 1988.

Block, Peter. *Stewardship: Choosing Service Over Self-Interest*. San Francisco: Berrett-Koehler, 1993.

Bloom, Allan. *The Closing of the American Mind*. New York: Simon & Schuster, 1987.

Brown, W. Stephen. *13 Fatal Errors Managers Make and How You Can Avoid Them*. New York: Berkley Books, 1988.

Bruner, Jerome. *On Knowing: Essays for the Left Hand*. New York: Atheneum Books, 1962.

Burns, James McGregor. *Leadership*. New York: Harper Torchbooks, 1978.

Carse, James P. *Finite and Infinite Games*. New York: Free Press, 1986.

Clemens, John K., and Douglas F. Mayer. *The Classic Touch: Lessons in Leadership from Homer to Hemingway*. Homewood, Ill.: Dow Jones-Irwin, 1987.

Covey, Steven R. *Principle Centered Leadership*. New York: Simon & Schuster, 1990.

———. *The Seven Habits of Highly Effective People*. New York: Simon & Schuster, 1989.

Daloz, Laurent A., et al. *Common Fire: Leading Lives of Commitment in a Complex World*. Boston: Beacon Press, 1997.

Deal, Terrance, and Allen Kennedy. *Corporate Cultures*. Reading, Mass.: Addison-Wesley, 1982.

DePree, Max. *Leadership Is an Art*. New York: Doubleday, 1989.

————. *Leadership Jazz*. New York: Doubleday, 1992.

Drucker, Peter. *The Age of Discontinuity*. New York: Harper & Row, 1969.

————. *Managing for the Future: The 1990s and Beyond*. New York: Truman Talley Books, 1992.

Ferguson, Marilyn. *The Aquarian Conspiracy*. Los Angeles: Tarcher, Inc., 1980.

Freedman, Samuel G. *Small Victories*. New York: Harper & Row, 1989.

Gardner, Howard, et al. *Good Work: When Excellence and Ethics Meet*. New York: Basic Books, 2001.

Gardner, John. *On Leadership*. New York: Free Press. 1990.

Gelb, Michael. *How to Think Like Leonardo Da Vinci*. New York: Dell, 1998.

————. *The How to Think Like Leonardo Da Vinci Workbook*. New York: Dell, 1999.

Gelb, Michael J., and Tony Buzan. *Lessons from the Art of Juggling*. New York: Harmony Books, 1994.

Golding, William. *Lord of the Flies*. New York: Capricorn Books, 1959.

Goodlad, John. *Teachers for Our Nation Schools*. San Francisco: Jossey-Bass, 1990.

Griffith, Samuel B. *Sun Tzu: The Art of War*. New York: Oxford University Press, 1971.

Heisenberg, Werner. *Physics and Philosophy*. New York: Harper, 1958.

Helgesen, Sally. *The Female Advantage: Women's Ways of Leadership*. New York: Doubleday Currency, 1990.

Hickman, Craig R. *Mind of a Manager; Soul of a Leader*. New York: Wiley, 1990.

Jaworski, Joseph. *Syncronicity: The Inner Path of Leadership*. San Francisco: Berrett-Koehler, 1996.

Keegan, John. *The Masks of Command*. New York: Viking Press, 1987.

Kidder, Tracy. *Among School Children*. Boston: Houghton Mifflin, 1989.

Koestenbaum, Peter. *Leadership: The Inner Side of Greatness*. San Francisco: Jossey-Bass, 1991.

Kouzes, James M., and Barry Z. Posner. *The Leadership Challenge*. San Francisco: Jossey-Bass, 1987.

Kushel, Gerald. *Reaching the Peak Performance Zone*. New York: Amacom, 1994.

Machiavelli, Nicolo. *The Prince and the Modern Discourses*, with an introduction by Max Lerner. New York: Modern Library, 1940.

McCormack, Mark H. *What They Don't Teach You at the Harvard Business School*. New York: Bantam Books, 1984.

Melville, Herman. *Billy Budd, Sailor (An Inside Narrative)*. Chicago: University of Chicago Press, 1962.

Morgan, Gareth. *Riding the Waves of Change: Developing Managerial Competencies for a Turbulent World*. San Francisco: Jossey-Bass, 1988.

Mortimer, Peter, et al. *School Matters*. Berkeley: University of California Press, 1988.

Moss-Kanter, Rosabeth. *The Change Masters*. New York: Simon & Schuster, 1983.

Moxley, Russ S. *Leadership as Spirit: Breathing New Vitality and Energy into Individuals and Organizations*. San Francisco: Jossey-Bass, 2000.

Moyers, Bill. *A World of Ideas: Conversations with Thoughtful Men and Women About American Life Today and the Ideas Shaping Our Future*. New York: Doubleday, 1989.

Musashi, Miyamoto. *The Book of Five Rings: The Real Art of Japanese Management*. New York: Bantam Books, 1982.

Naisbitt, John. *Megatrends*. New York: Warner Books, 1982.

Olson, Robert W. *The Art of Creative Thinking: A Practical Guide*. New York: Barnes & Noble, 1978.

Papert, Seymour. *Mindstorms*. New York: Basic Books, 1980.

Patterson, Jerry, et al. *Productive School Systems for a Nonrational World*. Alexandria, Va.: Association for Supervision and Curriculum Development, 1980.

Peters, Tom. *Liberation Management: Necessary Disorganization for the Nanosecond Nineties*. New York: Fawcett Columbine, 1992.

Peters, Tom, and Nancy Austin. *Passion for Excellence*. New York: Warner Books, 1986.

———. *Thriving on Chaos*. New York: Knopf, 1987.

———. *The Tom Peters Seminar*. New York: Vintage Books, 1994.

Peters, Thomas J., and Robert H. Waterman, Jr. *In Search of Excellence*. New York: Warner Books, 1982.

Pirsig, Robert M. *Zen and the Art of Motorcycle Maintenance*. New York: Bantam Books, 1981.

Rehfeld, John E. *Alchemy of a Leader*. New York: Wiley, 1994.

Roberts, Wes. *The Leadership Secrets of Attila the Hun*. New York: Warner Books, 1987.

Schon, Donald A. *The Reflective Practitioner*. New York: Basic Books, 1983.

Schumacher, E. F. *Good Work*. New York: Harper & Row, 1979.

Sculley, John. *Odyssey, Pepsi to Apple . . . A Journey of Adventure, Ideas, and the Future*. New York: Harper & Row, 1987.

Senge, Peter M. *The Fifth Discipline: The Art and the Practice of the Learning*

Organization. New York: Doubleday Books, 1990.

Sergiovanni, Thomas J. *Moral Leadership: Getting to the Heart of School Improvement.* San Francisco: Jossey-Bass, 1992.

Shakeshaft, Carol. *Women in Educational Administration.* Newbury Park, Calif.: Sage, 1989.

Shakespeare, William. *Henry V.* New York: Washington Square Press, 1989.

Siser, Theodore. *Horace's Compromise.* Boston: Houghton Mifflin, 1985.

Sloma, Richard S. *No Nonsense Management.* New York: Bantam Books, 1981.

Smith, Page. *Killing the Spirit.* New York: Viking Penguin Books, 1990.

Sophocles. *Antigone.* New York: Washington Square Press, 1970.

Turkle, Sherry. *The Second Self.* New York: Simon & Schuster, 1984.

van Oech, Roger. *A Kick in the Seat of the Pants.* New York: Harper & Row, 1986.

————. *A Whack on the Side of the Head.* New York: Warner Books, Inc., 1983.

Waitley, Dennis. *Empires of the Mind: Lessons to Lead and Succeed in a Knowledge-Based World.* New York: Morrow, 1995.

Wheatley, Margaret. *Leadership and the New Science: Learning About Organization from an Orderly Universe.* San Francisco: Berrett-Koehler, 1992.

Wheatley, Margaret, and Myron Kellner-Rogers. *A Simpler Way.* San Francisco: Berrett-Kochler, 1998.

About the Author

Raymond Lemley is passionate about schools and about the men and women who lead them. When you ask him what his favorite job has been, he will emphatically state: "Being a principal." Dr. Lemley has devoted the majority of his career to serving as a principal, training principals, and working on behalf of principals. He has also taught English at the high school and college levels and kindergarten at an inner-city school.

Dr. Lemley was principal for twelve years at Daniel Hand High School in Madison, Connecticut. In his position at the National Association of Secondary School Principals as administrator of training and later as deputy executive director, he worked with K–12 principals throughout the United States. He also served as the first executive director of the Texas Principals Leadership Initiative.

He was a member of the Educational Leadership faculty at Northern Arizona University and served as chair of that department during his tenure. Dr. Lemley is currently teaching leadership classes at the University of South Florida in Lakeland, Florida and is a partner in Leadership Training Associates in Marco Island, Florida. His professional interests remain focused on the principalship.